IT'S A SIN TO TELL A LIE

MARTY GROSZ

It's a Sin to Tell a Lie
MY LIFE IN JAZZ

with Joe Plowman

Golden Alley Press
Emmaus, Pennsylvania

In this work, the author has tried in good faith to recreate real events, locales, and conversations from his memories of them. The conversations in the book do not necessarily represent word-for-word transcripts. They are essentially accurate retellings meant to evoke the feeling and meaning of what was said. In the spirit of our commitment to publishing works of quality and integrity, Golden Alley Press offers this book to our readers. However, the stories, experiences, and words are the author's alone.

Golden Alley Press
37 S. Sixth Street
Emmaus, PA 18049

www.goldenalleypress.com

The text of this book is set in Minion
Book designed by Michael Sayre

Printed in United States of America
1 3 5 7 9 10 8 6 4 2

It's a Sin to Tell a Lie / Marty Grosz with Joe Plowman

Library of Congress Control Number: 2020931066

ISBN 978-1-7333055-3-2 Print
ISBN 978-1-7333055-4-9 eBook

Front and back cover images courtesy of the author's private collection

Cover design by Michael Sayre

To great-aunt Tali

and

onkel Viktor and his wife tante Claire

CONTENTS

FOREWORD

I met Marty when I was 23, fresh out of music school. My only
ambitions were to play the bass well, thump out good quarter
notes, shine in every band I played in, and – most importantly –
pay the rent. I knew more old-time jazz tunes than your average
millennial, but my knowledge of jazz history tapered off somewhere about the mid-1940s.

Then came the summer of 2014. One night I was playing
a walking bass line solo over a chorus of "Avalon." The band I
was with seemed to be feeling it, and the face of our trombonist,
Panic Slim – a.k.a. Jim Gicking, snapped towards me with a "We
should talk later" sort of grin.

Later that evening Slim rattled off a list of names: Steve
Brown. Eddie Condon. Eddie Lang. And Marty Grosz, living
legend, residing right here in Philadelphia. Did I know of them?
Never having heard these names, I naturally said, "Sure, I know
them all!"

Slim eventually discovered my ignorance and decided I
must become acquainted with Marty Grosz – and fill the recently
vacated bass chair in his band. Soon I was booked to play my first
show with Marty's band in Philadelphia. As instructed, I called
him to get my bearings, musically and otherwise.

The amount of information Marty gave me in our first call
was staggering. It felt like four semesters of jazz history condensed

into in two hours. I jotted notes while he talked: names of bassists, band leaders, composers, song titles, all from the 1920s and '30s. It was the perfect time in my life to be given the task of mining, digesting, and presenting this rich material to an audience. But in time for the weekend's gig? I got to work studying and practicing.

Panic Slim also tasked me with driving Marty to and from his various concerts and gigs. I accepted, figuring time would tell if I'd been conscripted because of my bass playing or my access to my girlfriend's (now wife's) car.

Years later, I can now say that working with Marty has taught me more than I even know. He taught me to appreciate the beauty of the songwriting of the '20s and '30s. As a bassist, there is great professional value in internalizing a vast number of "American songbook" standards. With my newfound appreciation for the older side of the repertoire, new paths were opened to me, especially with players of the earlier jazz styles.

Through years of traveling to gigs together, sharing meals, hanging after shows, and hearing his shtick between songs, Marty's bandmates and I began collecting his stories. These yarns are fascinating windows into the showbiz world of the early 20th century. As anyone who has heard him knows, Marty owns these stories because he carved out a career for himself amongst jazz's most well-known players.

There are two parts to this book.

Part One is Marty's story, written in his own words. True to form, he wrote the original manuscript out longhand, in two spiral-bound notebooks.

Part Two is a compilation of interviews with Marty that I recorded in South Philadelphia between 2015 and 2019. Once I started hearing his stories, told as only Marty can tell them, I knew that this oral history needed to be preserved. I used the earliest material as a term final for my master's degree. The rest came about four years later. Arranged loosely by subject matter, they represent a distillation of Marty's best material. His voice really shines through: vintage Marty.

Joe Plowman
Philadelphia, Pennsylvania
2020

Joe Plowman, editor of the Jazz Story Club series, is a musician in Philadelphia. With a Master of Music degree from Temple University, he tours nationally and internationally and holds the bass chair in many Philadelphia area bands, including that of Marty Grosz.

PART I

My Story

Young Marty with father, George Grosz

CHAPTER 1

Berlin Beginnings

I was born in 1930 in Berlin, Germany. My father was German artist George Grosz, famous for his caricatures and paintings that evidenced his disdain for the ruling class, bourgeoisie, militarism and capitalism during the Weimar Republic in the 1920s.

My father, mother, Eva (nee Peter), brother, Peter (born 1926), and I lived in a comfortable, roomy apartment near the heart of Berlin.

My mother said that I was a late talker. After many months of producing little more than blips and blurps, so I was told, my parents had begun to despair that I would ever form intelligible words, let alone enunciate the names "Mama" and "A'a," which momentarily assure parents that the production of offspring was worth the effort. Then one day, for some reason, I began to blab and haven't stopped blabbing since.

When I was in grade school, I concocted puns and riddles that went on forever. My mother claimed I had a case of "talkitis." Over the years I've been guilty of inducing more than my fair share of terminal boredom cases, for which I apologize. It's as if I've never stopped trying to play catch-up.

My parents met when the first World War had broken out, a time when the art movement called Dada had taken hold in Berlin. Grosz made Dada poems, made Dada collages, and took part in Dada cabaret performances. One Dada cabaret moment that he remembered was when he ate his black bowtie – it was licorice – while my mother stood me on a ladder and I emptied a bucket of shredded newsprint on his head.

They thrived in Berlin. *Vati* (Daddy) was well known in the city's art world, esteemed for his large canvases that depicted the chaos of big-city life and indicted the German ruling class. He was equally celebrated for his acerbic pen-and-ink drawings that skewered the manners and morals of the bourgeoisie and was in demand for designing theater sets and costumes.

For my parents, Berlin was the perfect place to be, a thriving metropolis on par with Paris, London, and New York City, humming with innovative music, art, literary, and political activity. We lived in a roomy, high-ceilinged middle-Europa apartment in a comfortable neighborhood. My mother, a superb cook and hostess, sewed many of her own clothes, with the result that she stayed "chic," without spending a small fortune on dresses.

While I gurgled in my playpen, the flimsy fabric of German democracy, the *Weimar Republik,* was unravelling under the pressure of wild inflation and huge reparations imposed by the victors of the World War, namely France, England, and Italy.

Frequent turmoil between cadres of "Brownshirts" (Nazis), and "Reds" (Communists) took place in Berlin, Hamburg, Köln, Munich, and lesser cities. A state of apprehension and insecurity pervaded throughout Germany.

George Grosz was a particular target of Nazi venom. Throughout the 1920s his satirical cartoons had attacked the German military and oligarchy, lampooned the captains of industry, and even depicted Hitler as a feeble, bearskin-clad tenor in some Wagnerian opera, carrying a spear and wearing a helmet bearing cow horns. Needless to say, Grosz's acerbic sketches did not endear him to the Nazis.

On one occasion a gang of them came to his studio to teach him a lesson, shouting "Where is Grosz, the Yiddish sow (*Saujude*)?" *Sau* is, of course, female in German, but it is gender-equal when used as a term of opprobrium.

Although I never knew them to be church-goers, my parents were born into the state religion, Lutheranism, as were the majority of Germans. Jews had long been assimilated into German society, as they had been in other European nations such as Holland and England.

Tyrants require enemies and scapegoats, real or imagined, to establish and maintain their power. Hitler and his Nazis sensed what would work for them, so they picked the old targets: Jews, homosexuals, gypsies, Seventh-Day Adventists, union organizers, and communists, to name a few. Once again, the word "Jude" (new) was fashioned into a term of opprobrium.

My father managed to evade a certain drubbing from the Nazi yobs by appearing at his studio door in his painting clothes:

3

paint-bespattered shirt, tattered trousers, a cleaning rag in one hand and a broom in the other, explaining that he was just a fellow who came once a week to tidy up the studio and was just leaving. Whereupon he slammed the studio door shut, leaving the rowdies to find someone else to pick on. A fortunate escape this time, but a disquieting portent of things to come.

Just for the record, we were not Jewish. My father, not a man to grow excited and lose his composure in daily life, would become visibly angry and excoriate persons who used anti-Semitic slogans or sang mocking ditties.

1930 ushered in more incidents of violence between the Nazis and the Reds. As street battles increased, so did my parents' apprehension about the possibility of enjoying a safe future in Berlin.

The more the Nazis castigated Grosz, the more nervous my family became. Some relatives argued that we should remain in the Fatherland, confident that the new regime would, in a rare show of magnanimity, welcome us to the "new order." How anyone of sound mind could suppose that a pack of brutal, immoral, deceitful opportunists would welcome a well-known antagonist into their fold is beyond comprehension.

As the political skies darkened, a bolt from the blue. On April 26th, 1932, George Grosz received a telegram from New York's Art Students League inviting him to teach a summer course. The invitation resulted from a sit-down strike by the students. They wanted teachers who were more in tune with the times, more politically aware than their current instructors.

On June 3rd, 1932, George Grosz disembarked in New York City. During his stay he was feted by fellow artists and the art community. Years later he told me of his adventures during this period. One event that stuck in my head was when he was invited to a party at a Fifth Avenue mansion. Liquor was flowing, a piano thumping, and the guests wanted to dance. Whereupon several gentlemen began to roll up the carpet until they found themselves blocked by a fellow who was passed out in an over-stuffed chair. Rather than try to wake the toper, they carried him in his chair into an adjoining room, where he continued his alcoholic stupor. Who was this elegant inebriate? None other than composer George Gershwin, a Grosz admirer who had consulted with him about taking painting lessons.

Grosz's stay in New York was a success. He received excellent coverage from the press, and he made some lifelong friends, one being Erich Cohn, a patron of German artists who had left their country to avoid Nazi persecution. Cohn, the CEO of a pasta factory, would often help our family when we were in financial straits later.

Vati returned to Berlin in early October 1932. My parents set to work packing up our furniture, clothing, books, and Vati's artwork. He had saved everything. Not only were large oil paintings packed into crates, but also his brushes, pens, pencils, crayons, easels: everything.

In mid-January 1933, my parents embarked for the United States, leaving brother Peter and me with Great Aunt "Tali." My mother would come back and fetch us once she and Vati were established in New York. Tali's husband had died in the great flu epidemic that had ravaged Europe and America at the end of the World War. Although she had none of her own, Tali was good with children. She took us on walks exploring Berlin's museums, its zoo, and especially its new art-deco airport at Tempelhof. She owned a large Mercedes convertible in which she took Peter and me for rides, after which she would give us wizened brown bananas that had been dried on her windowsills. To me they tasted like candy.

My parents departed Germany in mid-January 1933. Hitler became chancellor on January 30th. One day later, Nazi troopers stormed into our apartment on Trautenaustrasse and raided my father's studio on Nassauische Strasse. They found nothing of value or interest. Peter and I were housed incognito with Great Aunt Tali, while Vati and Mutti were looking for a place to rent in the vicinity of Manhattan.

Shortly after Hitler's assumption of power, George Grosz was branded a *Staatsfeind* (enemy of the state), as far as we know, one of the first, if not *the* first, artist/intellectual to be designated as such. Staatsfeind had his assets seized, his citizenship voided, and his passport taken away. But Grosz had been too quick for the Nazis: he had cleaned out his assets before the new administration could get ahold of them.

In October of 1933, Mutti returned to bring Peter and me over to the United States. We sailed on the *SS Bremen*, which was the size of a large hotel. It was the best trip I ever took, the choppy North Atlantic notwithstanding. It boasted a playroom for children, a movie theater with cartoon programs, a biddies' barbershop; in short, all the amenities for young travelers.

When the *Bremen* was about two days from its destination, a mail plane, an open-cockpit, single-propeller, pontoon-shaped biplane, was catapulted from the deck. It was stuffed with canvas bags filled with airmail letters. The seaplane would arrive in

New York City two days before the regular mail that the liner was carrying.

Upon approaching the American coast, our liner was surrounded by seabirds scavenging for bits of food. Passengers tossed morsels of bread from the decks; the birds caught every crumb. Then, through the mist, we glimpsed the southern coastline of Long Island. As we neared the port of New York, the *Ambrose* lightship, a permanently-anchored crimson sloop, indicated the proximity of the Verrazano Narrows. After passing through this bottleneck, our ship came to a complete stop to take aboard the pilot who would guide us into its berth on the west side of Manhattan.

The harbor teemed with boats of every description: freighters, tankers, fireboats, garbage scows, barges loaded with sand or gravel, ferries, police boats, excursion boats that would take you on a tour of New York Harbor for a dollar, and private pleasure craft whose passengers waved whiskey bottles to celebrate the end of Prohibition.

After passing the Statue of Liberty, Pete and I stood at the railing, awe-struck by Manhattan's skyscrapers and the clever manner in which the tugboats shoehorned us into the *Bremen*'s berth on the West Side.

CHAPTER 2

New York to Berlin and Back

For a week or two, we stayed at a hotel on Central Park West, an area where the fees were quite reasonable, and a sizeable number of Middle-Europa émigrés had settled. It was during this brief stay that I first experienced the allure of applause. I had been given colored chalk with which to draw on sidewalks. My decoration of walkways in Central Park attracted onlookers who would clap after I rose from my knees. Heady stuff.

Sometimes the family, all four of us, would walk across Central Park to Fifth Avenue to visit my father's stepsister, Tante Claire, and her husband who my brother and I called "Onkel" Viktor. His full name was Viktor Steiner. Before the turn of the nineteenth century he had studied at Heidelberg University in Germany and had the dueling scars to verify his status as one of the "elite" students. After graduation he studied to be a physician, eventually becoming a prominent gynecologist and teacher, qualified to treat the family of Kaiser Wilhelm, though it is doubtful that he ever raised the hem of a royal gown. But this is only conjecture on my part; his impeccable manners would not have allowed him to reveal the names of his patients. In World War I, he held the rank of major and commanded an army hospital.

One of my earliest Berlin memories is of Doktor Steiner's manservant, Fritz, carrying me up the stairs to their apartment. Later I would learn that Onkel Viktor and Tante Claire lived in an elegant art deco building. It survived the Word War II bombings and is now a high-end hotel.

Viktor's wife, Claire, my father's half-sister, was older than my father, of whom she was fond. She and her sister Martha grew up in Stolp, in eastern Pomerania on the Polish border. There, my grandfather, who died in 1905, ran an *Offizierskasino*, a sort of men's club for the aristocratic officers of a cavalry regiment. Somehow Claire found her way to Berlin and into the fashion business, working her way up to head buyer of women's fashions at Berlin's largest and most-esteemed department store: the KDW, short for *Kaufhaus des Westons* (Department Store of the West).

In New York, now and then, Onkel Viktor and Tante Claire would babysit me. After I was tucked into bed, I would marvel at the noises of the big city. I thought their apartment was huge: one could have roller skated from the front door to the dining room. Viktor and Claire were somewhat stuffy but exceedingly well-mannered. At dinner finger bowls would be furnished.

As I grew older, I wondered where their money came

from. I often wanted to ask but forbore. Much later, after they had both died, I learned that Onkel Viktor's family, S.S. Steiner, were the leading hops brokers in the world. Onkel Viktor's older brother, Sam, was connected to Col. Jake Ruppert, who produced Ruppert's Beer and Rheingold Beer, both major sellers in the New York area. For many years, Jake Ruppert owned the New York Yankees baseball team, for which he had built Yankee Stadium.

Whenever I spent a few days at the Fifth Avenue apartment, Onkel Viktor would take me to a museum or the zoo. Several times we went to one of the large movie theaters in the Times Square area. In those days, theaters showed a movie but also had vaudeville acts. It was at the Roxy that I watched a banjo player do an act which largely consisted of him strumming a peppy tune and getting more and more tangled up as he went along. First one leg would start stomping in time with the tune he was picking. He would talk and pound the leg down. Launching into the tune again, his other leg would start stomping, forcing him to tamp that one A satisfied grin on his face, he resumed. This time the legs kept still, but his arms started flapping, and so forth. At the conclusion of his turn, he played a piece all the way through without interruption. I was transfixed. I must have been about 8 or 9 years old, and somehow the metallic sound the banjo player produced got into my cortex. But I digress.

After a couple of weeks, we moved from the hotel to Bayside, Long Island, into a rented house on the corner of several acres of lawn and trees that were part of an estate belonging to an elderly woman. Our house was close to the Long Island Railroad track. Ever since, I've liked living near the sound of trains.

Brother Pete was enrolled in P.S.41, and I was placed into a kindergarten run by a lady with a large touring car in which she would drive us to a beach on a woodland trail. The first American song I can remember is "Lazy Bones," probably because of the image of bones napping under a tree.

Pop went into Manhattan to teach about three days a week and spent time at home drawing illustrations for various magazines and painting pictures which he sold through a New York City gallery. We lived modestly but comfortably. We even had a second-hand Willys-Knight sedan, which Mom drove. Pop never got the hang of driving. Oma (Grannie) Peter came over for a visit, carrying gifts for everyone, including a supply of highly malodorous German cheese which permeated her clothing. I can recall her in a borrowed bathrobe sniffing her blouses and skirts that were being aired in the sun.

In 1935, we took a trip back to Europe, this time on a freighter which had accommodations for about 40 or 50 passengers. Pete and I had a great time. Since there were no class restrictions as on the large liners, we could roam all over the ship. The crew let us visit the engine room, we climbed into lifeboats, and the radioman let me tap a telegraph key. Because of his "Enemy of the State" status, Pop couldn't go to Berlin with us. He stayed in Holland with a Dutch painter, a friend from his art-student days in Dresden. By then we had all applied for U.S. passports. American citizenship required five years residence in the U.S.

At a party at Oma's apartment in Berlin, I was designated to "rush the growler," that is, to go downstairs to the restaurant and come back with a pitcher of beer. Of course, an adult accompanied me. So why do I remember this trivial event? I suppose because it made me feel important and older, especially when I returned with the goods intact.

After Berlin, there was a family reunion at the Danish island of Bornholm. On the way home, we traveled through Denmark proper. I still have the impression of meeting Bertolt Brecht, the author of the famous *Threepenny Opera* and lyricist of "Mack the Knife." Pop knew him quite well because they had shared political viewpoints and because Pop had provided set and scenery designs for Brecht. Again, why do I remember meeting this person? The reason, I think, is because when he met us at his door, he was dressed in an American railroad engineer's jacket, and had his hair cut in bangs. Clothes make the man.

George and Eva Grosz

CHAPTER 3

American Life

The following year we moved about four miles further east to Douglaston, where my parents rented a somewhat larger house with a garage for our second-hand Buick. A one-lane road separated our front lawn from a slight drop that led to Little Neck Bay, where on weekends dozens of men would dig clams. Pete and I were enrolled in P.S.98, a fifteen-minute walk from our house.

Like many transplants, we spoke our native tongue at home and English in public. English words like which, what, and weather often came out as *vitch*, *vaht*, and *wezzer* when spoken by Germans. Sometimes Mom and Pop and German friends would practice their pronunciation by articulating words like these in front of a candle. They would know if they were succeeding if they blew out the flame. Mom and Pop were giving themselves a crash course by listening to the radio and trying to figure out why audiences were laughing at jokes that they didn't understand. Brother Pete and I understood the kid shows like *Jack Armstrong, the All-American Boy* and *The Lone Ranger*, but we eschewed the adult soap operas and comedy shows.

During the 1930s we were visited by a succession of Pop's friends and cronies who had left Germany, often by tortuous routes. Since Pop had a steady job teaching and was enhancing his income by selling a picture now and then and furnishing illustrations for magazines, he showed enough income to be able to vouch for his émigré friends.

Now and then Mom and Pop and an "old country" crony would sit up all night in our kitchen arguing about European politics mostly, Pop trying to convince his friends that just because Hitler and his Nazis were evil, it didn't therefore make Stalin and his Reds any less vicious.

Pop sent Pete and me off to the community church every Sunday. When I asked him why we had to attend these dull, boring services to listen to the minister's monotone sermons and join in the listless hymn singing, he explained that when he left Germany behind, he wanted all of us to become "Americans," not immigrants who yearn to return to the old country and complain that nothing in their adopted land can surpass the cooking, the tailoring, the music, the manners, the intellectual atmosphere of the land they had to leave behind.

One Christmas during the War, Mom and Pop invited a group of guests, fugitives from Europe, loners, émigrés. They fed them a Christmas dinner of middle-Europa soul food: goose, red cabbage, and plenty of *sekt* (German champagne). Mom played them Richard Tauber singing "*Stille Nacht, Heilige Nacht*" on the phonograph, and sooner or later the guests would get maudlin as the bubbly did its work. And of course, they would speak longingly of the old country, the good old days in the *Heimat* (homeland) where everything looked better, sounded better, tasted better. Alas, that, in the days before television, is what people did at Christmas. They ate too much, drank too much, and grew misty-eyed and maudlin. I can still see Pop sloshing down the after-dinner brandy, growing red in the face.

And then: boom! He banged his glass on the table and lit into the sad guests, roaring, "YOU SMALL-MINDED NOBODIES! You should kiss the American soil you walk on. You ingrates, if it weren't for the benevolence of the U.S.A., you'd be starving, or suffering in concentration camps, or dead!" These tirades were delivered in German, which is a particularly effective language for angry tirades.

Wartime saw several outbursts of this type. When I was 11, or 12, or 13, I would retreat to the kitchen. Mom, of course, would understand the situation and sympathize with Pop. Her sisters, their husbands, and our cousins were getting the "bejabbers" bombed out of themselves in Berlin. They weren't members of the Nazi Party, nor did they have the opportunity or wherewithal to relocate to another country, let alone to a rural community. Bombs have no conscience.

CHAPTER 4

Swing

In 1942, the landlord had our furnace converted from oil to coal. This was in keeping with the oil shortage caused by the need for fuel for the war effort. One of my chores was to clean the furnace and shovel out the clinkers, which we kept for placing under our car's wheels in icy conditions. One Saturday I noticed Pop stacking logs and newspaper in our living room fireplace. When I asked him why, he replied that he thought it would create a cozy atmosphere for a potential customer who was being driven from New York City to look at paintings. We had lived in this house for more than five years but never used the fireplace.

While I was busy making my bed and mopping the bathroom floor to prepare for our visitor, I became aware of smoke rolling up the stairs. I raced down and saw Pop dumping a pitcher of water on the logs. Smoke had permeated the place. Windows were opened and we frantically waved towels and newspapers to push the smoke out, turning the house into a refrigerated meat locker. Once fairly rid of smoke, it was slow to warm up. We donned sweaters and scarves and drank coffee. My parents were city people, and it had never occurred to them that our chimney, after many years of being idle, could have benefitted from a visit by a chimney sweep.

Once the potential calamity was brought under control, I asked who this guest was, that we needed to have a fire for. Pop replied that his agent was bringing Artie Shaw and his latest wife, Kathleen Winsor.

Artie Shaw? I was thunderstruck. Artie Shaw was a top swing band leader with a roster of hits: "Begin the Beguine," "Stardust," "Frenesi," and on and on. And even I knew that Kathleen Winsor was a pert, sexy young lady who had written a huge bestseller, a bodice-buster called *Forever Amber*. When they finally showed up, late, I, of course, stayed out of the way. I did manage to get Shaw's autograph inside a matchbook cover.

The next morning, I awoke to hear my mother excoriating Shaw in German. It seems that Shaw had availed himself of the toilet, smoked a cigarette, and while doing so placed the butt on the pyralin lid of the bathroom hamper – thus burning a small, dark trench into the lid. The hamper had to be retired to invalid status in the laundry room. The following Monday I showed Artie's autograph to classmates. They didn't believe it was genuine.

Brother Pete had built himself a radio that could receive all sorts of hard-to-find stations. Now and then he'd let me come into his room and listen. In return, I would draw cartoons for him.

With the onset of puberty, I became interested in jazz, although it was called "swing" then.

By the late 1930s, America's youth was infatuated with swing music. It's difficult to define swing precisely, but in the twenties and thirties, ballrooms and dance halls sprang up all over America. Hundreds of dance bands, orchestras of usually 14 musicians or more, crisscrossed the country playing in these ballrooms. These groups made thousands of 78 rpm recordings and flourished from roughly 1930 until 1950, a period known as the swing era. They were known as "swing" bands, to distinguish them from "sweet" bands.

The word swing also described an infectious rhythmic pulse that would get feet tapping and stimulate the dancers. Needless to say, certain players were more adept at creating this groove than others. One of the first musicians to catch my attention was pianist Thomas "Fats" Waller, who generated excitement, swing, and had a beat that could make a mummy dance. Even his slower tempos would get feet tapping and bodies gyrating.

Waller was a master at producing mirth and feelings of happy abandon. He had a great asset in his ability to transform the most maudlin, silly songs into exciting vehicles for his improvisations and mocking asides. In addition to his talents as a superb pianist, organist, and vocalist, Waller composed an abundance of songs and piano pieces, many of which became standards: "Honeysuckle Rose," "Ain't Misbehavin'," "Keepin' Out of Mischief," "Squeeze Me," "My Fate is in Your Hands," "I've Got a Feeling I'm Falling," "Black and Blue," "I'm Crazy 'Bout My Baby," "The Jitterbug Waltz," "How Can You Face Me?" The list goes on.

That ponderous pachyderm of the piano, that elephantine
elf of the ivories, that caliph of the keys, that mastadon
of mirth, that emir of the escape tones, that sultan of the
Steinway, that bwana of the Bösendorfer, that pasha of
the pralltriller, that wazir of whoopie, that Hammurabi of
Hotcha, that guru of the grupettos, Thomas "Fats" Waller.
© 1933 Frank Driggs Collection

Fats Waller and his Rhythm made scores of recordings in the '30s. It was a sextet consisting of trumpet, tenor sax (doubling clarinet), drums, bass, guitar, and, of course, piano. His guitarist, Al Casey, had started out with Fats as a teenager. Quite a few of the Rhythm's recordings featured acoustic chord-style solos by Casey.

By the time I slid into puberty, I was hooked. The amplified electric guitar had brazenly weaseled its way into jazz at the hands of Benny Goodman's guitarist Charlie Christian, the King Cole Trio's Oscar Moore, Chicago's George Barnes, and Waukesha's Les Paul. I regarded electric guitars as sounding "goopy" like electric organs. I much preferred, and still do, the tone of an acoustic steel-string guitar, which is what I heard on various radio shows. A good example: when Bing Crosby crooned a bit of his theme song "Where the Blue of the Night Meets the Gold the Day" at the start of his weekly radio program, accompanied by Perry Botkin on an acoustic Gibson L-5 guitar. I would sit through scores of corny *Fibber McGee and Molly* shows just to hear a few measures by the superb guitarist George Van Eps, who was in the studio orchestra.

Of course, guitarists jumped at the opportunity to make their instruments louder, and what started as a novelty became the norm. But before amplification took over, spawning all sorts of mayhem, the drums, piano, and bass had to lower their volume for a guitar solo to be heard. To me these moments were magical, similar to when a trumpeter inserts a mute, or a clarinetist solos in his lower register.

In 1942, the American Federation of Musicians, to which ninety-nine percent of professional musicians belonged, banned their members from participating in recording sessions unless

record producers contributed a percentage of their profits to
a musician's pension fund. The recording companies refused,
which resulted in a stalemate and a recording ban which lasted
until the Second World War's end. During the ban, several large
record producers initiated reissue programs, putting out albums
of jazz and dance music from the 1920s and 1930s.

While the union ban applied to union members only, e.g.
trumpeters, saxophonists, drummers, pianists, bass players, and
so on, vocalists were not considered musicians and were not
banned. All the stringed instruments were considered legitimate
and banned, except ukuleles. This situation resulted in a surfeit
of vocalists singing melodies backed by vocal groups intoning
harmonic lines, with the lower voices singing bass notes, and
several ukulele players plinking and plunking: a limited formula
at best.

In the 1940s, New York City boasted several independent
radio stations. Their disc jockeys played jazz, often emphasizing
the music that one couldn't hear on commercial radio, which
concentrated on hits by name artists.

The smaller stations presented programs of jazz from
the 1920s and '30s, enabling me to hear such exciting artists as
Bessie Smith, the fabulous blues singer; cornetist Bix Beiderbecke;
and clarinetists Jimmie Noone, Johnny Dodds, and Frank
Teschemacher. Add to that the seminal recordings of King Oliver
and Louis Armstrong, Jelly Roll Morton, The Duke Ellington
Orchestra, the stride pianists Fats Waller, James P. Johnson, Willie
"The Lion" Smith, and Joe Sullivan – the list goes on and on.

But back to puberty.

CHAPTER 5

First Guitar

I started attending jazz concerts at The Town Hall in New York in 1943. They were presented on Saturday afternoons; I could be home for supper. Many of the concerts were organized by guitarist Eddie Condon. Condon was a superb rhythm guitarist with an idiosyncratic style. The concerts were made up of small ensembles, piano features, a vocalist or two, and would end in a delirious cacophony played by all the musicians in a wild, improvised ensemble. At the same time, Condon emceed a weekly radio show that was beamed overseas to service personnel. It had much the same format as The Town Hall concerts.

Movie palaces on Broadway were presenting the leading swing attractions such as Benny Goodman, Count Basie, Duke Ellington, Artie Shaw, and Gene Krupa and their orchestras. If you got to the theater early, you paid a reduced admission price.

The big bands that were featured on live radio broadcasts, whose recordings were heard over and over on disc jockey shows, relied on proven commercial formulas, which left little room for improvised solos. Radio shows then, like television shows now, had to answer to their sponsors and their ratings, wherefore producers stuck mostly to what was safe and proven to succeed. Those audiences, just as today, wanted vocals, and that's what they got, with a few major exceptions such as Duke Ellington's "Mood Indigo" and "'A' Train," Benny Goodman's "Stompin' at the Savoy" and "Jersey Bounce," Count Basie's "One O'clock Jump," Artie Shaw's "Begin the Beguine," and Glenn Miller's "In the Mood."

For broadcast to service personnel, the government instituted V-Discs, both reissues of favorites and a rigorous program devoted to making new recordings for the troops. These were not made available to civilians.

I saved up money from my allowance, from gifts (instead of birthday and Christmas presents I would ask for donations), and from a summer job as a kitchen boy on Cape Cod. I spent most of my money on reissues of jazz records that had been made ten or fifteen years earlier, had been out of print, and had become collector's items. Many of the original pressings could be found at record stores specializing in collector's items, but they had become too expensive for me. The reissues cost the same as ordinary records. These reissues, which I could take into listening booths to sample, were miraculous revelations to me, striking me like a blast of fresh air. The music sounded raw, fervent, bursting with brilliant improvisations, though sometimes naïve in an exciting way.

All the rest of my spare change went into buying records of my favorite jazz musicians, particularly those featuring guitarists such as Eddie Lang, accompanying Joe Venuti; Al Casey, Fats Waller's guitarist; Teddy Bunn, a superior bluesman, and the fine rhythm players Allan Reuss and Eddie Condon. Not to mention the terrific chord stylings of Carl Kress and Dick McDonough.

I continued to luxuriate in the sounds of recordings from the '20s and '30s, seminal works by Louis Armstrong, Bix Beiderbecke, Jimmie Noone, Duke Ellington, McKenzie and Condon's Chicagoans, Eddie Lang, Fletcher Henderson, James P. Johnson, Willie "The Lion" Smith, Bunny Berigan, Fats Waller, Jack Teagarden, and hundreds more.

Somewhere along the way, I emptied my piggy bank and picked up a cheap wartime guitar. And I mean cheap. It had all the tone and resonance of a cardboard box; a toilet seat strung with dental floss would have sounded better. I picked and strummed to no avail, wherefore I purchased an even cheaper instrument, a sad-looking banjo. But at least I could get a tone out of it. After that, I made a point of asking professional players for advice on what guitar to buy. No two of them agreed. So, I kept buying and selling guitars until I found a winner.[1]

---

1 I now have just two fine instruments: a 1927 Gibson L-5 and a 1928 Gibson L-5. No pick-ups, no knobs, no gimmicks.

Prep School

In 1943, my parents and their American friends decided that it would be advantageous to all concerned if I followed in my brother's footsteps and attend his prestigious New England prep school. Both of our tuitions were guaranteed by Onkel Viktor and by scholarship grants. By the time I arrived at the academy, Pete had been drafted.

I was the target of flying dinner buns at my first meal in boarding school. Not knowing the etiquette of bread product propulsion, I returned the compliment: a response that seemed to mark me as an upstart. After dinner a pack of upperclassmen were waiting to teach me respect.

After bombarding me with salty billingsgate, they escorted me to a grassy knoll behind a senior dorm and proceeded to use me as tackling dummy. By this time, twenty or thirty students had gathered to witness my gradual dismemberment when, praise be! A fusillade of condoms filled with water wobbled through the air, dousing not only myself, but also the onlookers. This caused enough confusion that I was able to get back to my dorm without incident.

I arrived at my dorm only to find a vigorous chestnut fight between twenty or so freshmen was underway. Alas, more adolescent hijinks. I did not want to begin my stay at this hallowed institution giving the impression that I was a wimp, so I joined in the pointless fusillades. We didn't even know each other's names, and here we were aping what combatants all over the globe were doing with somewhat more lethal missiles.

The outcome? My chestnut smashed a lamp over the dorm's entrance. The tinkle of broken glass caused the housemaster to appear and ask the name of the culprit. I told him and he wrote it down. My first day: an omen?

The esteemed academy had for many years turned bumbling, unpolished, semi-literate whelps into socially acceptable young men who went on to become semi-literate college graduates. The schoolwork demanded writing in ink. Pencils could be used for notes. There were no true-or-false or multiple-choice answers. Ninety percent of assignments had to be fulfilled by the use of complete, grammatically correct sentences.

Although I have never looked back upon my three years there nor generated an atom of mist in my eyes by contemplating the pimply faces, loud farting, and jock behaviors, I applaud the school's emphasis on literacy. For some reason, writing came more easily to me than to many, which resulted in me always being chosen to participate in contests where I had to write essays about books – for example, on Dickens' *Martin Chuzzlewit* and the *American Notes*.

English Masters would press me to enter short story contests. I wrote gloop about jazz without really knowing anything about it. As often as possible, a couple of students and I would take the commuter train into Boston to see swing bands with an occasional visit to the Old Howard or Casino burlesque theaters.

The school at that time was all male. The closest one could get to the opposite sex was by attending an occasional Tea Dance at a nearby girls' academy. These dances were less exciting than bobbing for apples. Chaperones were stationed at the corners of the gym in which the dances were held lest one of the couples attempt body contact. If this was what polite society was like, then I wanted to join impolite society.

Summer vacation found me in Wellfleet, Massachusetts, on Cape Cod working as a kitchen boy. This meant I arrived at the "Holiday House" in mid-morning and worked until the last garbage can had been set outside, about 11 p.m. My salary was $15 per week. At the end of the summer I went back home and splurged most of it on records.

Back in boarding school, I escaped having to participate in team sports and their concomitant rah-rah mentality and the clichés of the formulaic pep talks given by coaches who yearned for early retirement. I signed up for general athletics, which meant I had to run laps in the gym, lift weights, and swing dumbbells.

New England prep schools acted as incubators for the offspring of the wealthy. My school had, for over a century, produced business leaders and politicians and trained young men to follow in their footsteps.

Students who were the scions of wealthy parents often exhibited what I would call imperious attitudes or behaviors, as if they knew that they were protected if they misbehaved. For example, "rich kids" would show up to be signed in at their dining hall at suppertime, and then leave to buy their own suppers at a nearby diner where they would buy hamburgers and milkshakes. One well-heeled student who never altered this supper menu was the cause of repeated toilet cloggings that necessitated visits from plumbers. Another classmate, whose father owned a chain of newspapers, would never avail himself of laundry services. Instead, he tossed his dirty shirts, underwear, and socks into his closet, giving them away to dorm mates after they were worn only once. Every week he made a trip to a local haberdasher to purchase replacements.

A classmate of mine whose family was one of the largest manufacturers of bathroom supplies, porcelain bathtubs, sinks, toilets, etc., tossed a lighted cherry bomb into a toilet in my "house," blowing the commode to smithereens. The students thought it was the coolest prank ever.

The annual football game with a rival academy found me dragooned into attending. I was never a sports fan, and riding in a bus to watch future board chairmen mangle one another was my idea of dullsville (contemporary hipster talk). But my compeers pressured me to go along. While on our rival's campus, a bunch of us entered the opposing locker room to use the toilets. On the way back out, a classmate picked up and handed me a tiny pennant with our rival's name on it.

"Here, take it," he said.

"What am I supposed to do with it?" I asked.

"Stick it on your wall, or stick it up your ass," he replied.

I kept the pennant and joined the throng headed for the football stadium. All boring things come to an end, don't they? Not in this case. At the daily assembly the next morning, the dean admonished us for the vandalism that too many students had engaged in, plundering our rivals, grabbing wrist watches, expensive fountain pens, neckties, sneakers, etc. All students would receive a document to be signed, stating that they had not taken part in the plundering.

I had accepted a tiny pennant, which meant nothing to me. So, I refused to sign. What could the school do, if I was to be punished for some petty theft? A few days later, exactly six students out of 300 were called to the Dean's office. There should have been 30 or more boys who plundered. Our punishment: probation, confined to school grounds.

I, for one, wasn't having it. On the following weekend, a friend and I took a bus to Boston and were spotted upon our return. On Monday, the dean gave us the boot. On the train ride to New York, I alternately sighed with relief and anxiety. What would my parents think?

Fortunately for me, they were understanding and seldom mentioned my "failure" to graduate from boarding school.

That year my parents decided it was time to stop renting and buy their own home. They found a place in Huntington, Long Island, a portion of a stable that had been remodeled into a dwelling. It was located near a mansion that stood on a hill in the middle of several acres of arable land, not far from an apple orchard.

The entire spread belonged to a man who had been in charge of the youth division of the German Communist Party. He had emigrated to America, renounced his previous affiliations, and was now a successful capitalist – a stock broker and a financier. His wife had enjoyed a successful acting career in Hungary and Austria. Now and then she would invite me to the mansion for tea.

Our house in the stable was a symphony in particle board. My room was over the kitchen so that the bass notes from my cheesy, "lo-fi" phonograph boomed loud enough to discombobulate my mother, a superior cook. Having been taught to honor my parents, especially the one that produced delicious meals, I erected a stack of books and towels upon which I placed my phonograph, effectively dampening the pounding.

When my parents entertained guests, I would be enlisted to help with dinner preparations. This duty would include helping my father to decant the wine, a task which involved uncorking bottles of Gallo Bros. "Vino di Tavola," one of the most inexpensive and unassuming red wines one could find. We called it "Vino Cheapo" and funneled it into bottles that my father had painted grapes and leaves and flowers upon. The sophisticated guests, most of whom moved in the artistic, literary, and cultural circles in Manhattan, guzzled the "Vino Cheapo" as if it had been supplied by Bacchus himself. When they asked Pop where he found this exhilarating elixir, he would wag a finger and exclaim, "That's my secret."

CHAPTER 7

Youthful Optimism

After my brother's discharge from the Navy, he joined us in Huntington. He and I painted our new home and dug our car out of a huge snowstorm. When spring came, he was off to work in a brewery and then to attend Harvard. That summer, I worked as a gofer for a summer theater, a job which included painting a large cyclorama. And then I enrolled at Huntington High School for my senior year.

High school was a relief after boarding school. The presence of girl students made a world of difference. Huntington was a fairly affluent town on the northside of Long Island, which meant the female students could afford to be turned out in fetching dresses, although sweaters and skirts were their customary school attire. It wouldn't have made any difference to me if they showed up in sackcloth and ashes.

Afternoons I would retreat into our garage to practice guitar. I made slow progress, doing many things wrong. I suppose I was headstrong. My parents were divided: Pop encouraged me; Mom thought I should take lessons. I avoided formal study because I sensed that a teacher would try to talk me into playing an amplified instrument and try to mold me into a "contemporary" player. But I didn't want that. I was fascinated with the sound of the pre-electric steel-string instrument. I did not like the hyped-up amplified sound that was all the rage. The charm of the pre-electric players was what I liked: the natural sound.

Both of my parents loved music in their own ways. Mom was tuned into WQXR, New York City's most prominent classical music station. While sewing her creations or cooking, she would sing along with Mozart, Schumann, Schubert, Jerome Kern, Porter, Beethoven, etc. Now and then, Pop would come up to my room and request a concert, which meant recordings. He would lie down on my bed, stare at the ceiling, and let the sounds of Louis Armstrong, Fats Waller, Duke Ellington, Eddie Lang, the Mound City Blue Blowers, Teddy Bunn, and Pee Wee Russell wash over him. Sometimes I would have to play a record over for him. They were 78 rpm records, which had a better, less compressed sound than the LPs would have.

In the years following the end of World War II, disc jockeys played less swing music and turned to featuring inane, almost childish songs such as "If I Knew You Were Comin' I'd've Baked a Cake," "They've Got an Awful Lot of Coffee in Brazil," "Buttons and Bows," and "It's Anybody's Spring." A slew of songs extolled the virtues of women in their post-war dream homes, cooking, baking, prettying themselves to greet their hubbies (understood to be ex-servicemen) at the front doors of their charming little bungalows while little Tommy and his sister Jane frolicked with their puppy, Spot. Television had not yet achieved its position as civilization's spellbinder.

Now and then I could take the train to Manhattan to meet up with young men my age to play hot music. Somehow, I had gotten rid of my orange-crate wood guitar and acquired an inexpensive four-string Gibson. I wanted a regular six-string instrument, but I didn't have enough money. For some reason, I was loath to ask my parents. Okay, so I'd start with four strings and as I improved, I'd move on to six strings. It's how many guitarists started out: playing four-string banjos in '20s dance bands, then switching to six-string guitars in the '30s. Somewhere along the way, I picked up a banjo. It cost me next to nothing because, with the advent of swing orchestras, guitars had replaced banjos in the rhythm sections.

In the mid-forties, the face of popular music was changing. Big bands were being challenged by small combos. Orchestra vocalists like Frank Sinatra, Perry Como, Ella Fitzgerald, and Kay Starr were appearing as singles. The era of "Stompin' at the Savoy" and "In the Mood" was ending. The era of bebop was in full swing. Younger jazz players were developing styles that emphasized technical virtuosity. Solos went on and on. The "boppers" felt that playing for dancers was beneath them. They were "artists," whatever that meant.

The implication was that they should be heard in concerts, and perhaps in jazz clubs playing for listeners who gave them their total attention, as if said listeners were hearing a piano recital by Rubinstein or violin concert by Heifetz.

Alas, jazz clubs depended on patrons who drank, who chatted up their dates, and who had no idea of what the musicians were up to. For the boppers, speed was the thing. They seldom just stated the melody of a piece simply and directly before transforming it into a wild, note-stuffed, double-time exercise, which imparted little soulfulness and much extravagant noodling.

In 1948, I ran into a boarding school buddy, Hugh McKay. Hugh was an aspiring clarinetist and free soul. By free soul I mean that he lived day-by-day and didn't seem to worry about tomorrow. He had spent his childhood in France where his father ran an advertising agency for American products. Hugh persuaded a couple of us amateur musicians to join him in Southampton, Long Island, where he had talked the owner of a Greek diner into employing a four-piece combo. No pay, but we would be put up in a defunct betting parlor, and we'd be fed. Ah, youth. We wanted to "tell our stories" (musician slang for playing a solo) and reckoned that our youthful exuberance would be enough to land us part-time day work mowing lawns, washing windows, whatever. Alas, gainful employment proved elusive.

I earned a few dollars by painting signs such as a farmer announcing a turkey shoot and a sign announcing a VFW dinner. After three weeks the job ended, and we returned to New York City. Hugh and I talked about our options: living at home, enrolling in some sort of school course, or working at menial jobs which adults claimed would build "character," whatever that meant.

The time had come to leave the nest and to try our luck in the cruel world. We had the optimism that comes when one reaches 18, the legal voting and drinking age in New York State.

CHAPTER 8

West to Chicago

We picked a Friday to head west. Our goal was to reach the West Coast and, you guessed it, Hollywood, where we imagined that our semi-wholesome good looks, our charm, and our radiant conversation could hardly fail to impress show-biz people, and one or both of us would wind up luxuriating among raven-tressed vixens in need of sympathy.

Hugh knew a girl who made us a couple of sandwiches. With a change of underwear stuffed into our instrument cases, clarinet, and guitar, we headed toward that gateway to the West, the Holland Tunnel. We had split a $10 bill, so with $5 each we set out to see the world, starting with America. In those days drivers picked up hitchhikers, and it wasn't long before a shoe salesman delivered us to somewhere in New Jersey, from whence we got rides to the Pennsylvania Turnpike, one of the few four-lane highways in those pre-interstate days. We got as far as Pittsburgh, where a boarding school pal put us up for the night.

From there, we managed to ride with truckers, mostly down two-lane highways through Ohio and Indiana. We didn't always get rides in the same truck but would meet up at a truck stop, where the drivers would buy us a meal. One trucker told me that he liked picking up passengers because they helped to relieve the monotony of long drives.

Grinding along through Indiana, one of our truckers encountered a car full of young men whose vehicle was weaving over the two-lane highway. After about twenty miles of alternately speeding and slowing, blocking our truck's passage, making faces, guffawing, and directing obscene gestures at our driver, they produced a rifle which they brandished out of their car window. At this point, the trucker's patience gave out. With a mighty roar of his engine, he pushed his gas pedal to the floor, bumped the lout's auto, and pushed it off the roadway into the mud and bushes that flanked it. A few hours later, our driver reached his destination, a steel mill in Gary. Here he wished us luck and handed us each a $5 bill, manna from heaven.

Looking back, I am amazed at the bravado we showed. Here we were trying to reach our first objective, Chicago, with no more than $10 between us.

A New York piano player had given me the name of Bob Lovett[1], a clarinetist who worked as a bartender at the University Tap on 57th Street next to the University of Chicago. It was evening by the time we reached him; he was working the bar. Hugh and I sat at a table nursing free beers until closing time. Bob put us up

---

1   Robert Q. Lovett later became a successful film editor for TV and movies. His work on *The Cotton Club* got him an Oscar nomination.

at his flat and helped us to find our way around the South Side of Chicago, where we found a cheap room with a couch and a bed. The next day we went to the Loop to answer a "Countermen Wanted" ad at Wimpy's, a chain of hamburger joints.

We reported to our respective locations. Of course, the pay was minimal, but the job came with one free meal. As a counterman, I picked up orders from the lady cooks and brought them to the customers. If they wanted a milkshake, I would make it. I developed a friendly relationship with the fat lady cooks, so they often provided my free hamburger with an extra meat patty while I dumped so much ice cream into my shake that the blender's blades would revolve at one-quarter speed.

Once in a while Bob Lovett would get me and/or Hugh on a gig: a student dance at the University of Chicago or a picnic, and I'd make a few bucks. I even managed to buy, from a pawnbroker, a $5 pin-striped suit that a Capone henchman might have worn.

After about a month at Wimpy's, I landed a job at the Carl Fischer music store on South Wabash Avenue. The pay was slightly better, and the working conditions were far better. I was a sales clerk, handyman, and stockman in the musical instrument department which sold saxophones, trumpets, clarinets, trombones, reeds, and all manner of musical accessories. My boss played the saxophone and understood musicians. My pal, Hugh, worked elsewhere in the store. We shared a cheap room on the Near North Side. Every evening one of us would sleep on the mattress of our one bed, while the other slept on the bedsprings insulated with newspapers. Breakfast was oatmeal cooked on a hot plate plugged into the dangling light socket. A cylindrical cardboard box of Quaker Oats cost twelve cents. Sugar came from drugstore lunch counters, water from the fetid communal bathroom down the hall.

When the Christmas season came around, I supplemented my meager income with temporary work for the postal service, unloading packages from boxcars into mail trucks. The hours were from 10 p.m. to 6 a.m., after which the janitor at my day job would let me in so I could get a couple of hours sleep propped up against a stack of saxophone cases before the store opened.

Was I happy? Indeed. There was much to learn, much to see, and I wasn't sitting in a classroom. Musician pals introduced me to a world that was tawdry but fascinating. I learned about a black boogie-woogie pianist named Jimmy Yancey who lived near 35th and State Street on the South Side. Jimmy had an unusual, almost pensive way of performing twelve-bar blues. He and his wife, known only as Mama, would hold monthly "rent" parties. Guests were asked to "feed the kitty" upon entering their railroad apartment. Soon the guests became animated. Jimmie would be coaxed into playing his old upright piano and Mama, a scrappy woman, would take over and croak her big number, "Death Letter Blues." "I received a letter" it began, slow and baleful. After another couple of slow blues, Mama would have me produce my guitar, and she would croak numbers that her husband didn't play, like "It's a Sin to Tell a Lie," or "Slow Boat to China."

Often well-known musicians dropped by after work, and the good times would roll. I can recall Albert Ammons, a powerful boogie-woogie artist, making the piano stomp. His son, Gene, played tenor sax. Gene was making a name in the bebop and rhythm and blues idioms. Don Ewell and George Zack took over keyboard duties and my pal Hugh would join in, as would Bob Lovett. As evenings wore on ladies would join the fun, doing bumps and grinds. A "collection" plate would make the rounds and fried chicken was sent for.

One night, while I was carrying a paper plate of chicken and potato salad, I needed to answer the call of nature. As I pushed open the bathroom door, there was Mama sitting on the commode.

"Oops, sorry," I said.

As I closed the door, a husky voice said, "Come on in, boy." It was Albert Ammons, his rotund body seated on the edge of the bathtub, conversing with Mama. I came in, stood by, holding my paper plate.

"That's good chicken, isn't it?" Mama said.

"Would you like some?" I asked, presenting my paper plate to both Mama and Albert.

"No thank you," was the reply, "but you go ahead."

CHAPTER 9

———————

The Victory Club

Bartender Bob Lovett introduced me to a dive on the Near North Side of Chicago called the Victory Club: a long bar and a little bandstand with a spinet piano. Over the bar were a row of bamboo monkey cages. At the end of the bar were the toilets. The urinals in the "Men's" were wired so that bells would ring when someone peed. The Victory Club appeared to be a haven for the restless, the lovers, and the kooks. Jazz music was supplied by a fine black trumpet player from New Orleans, Lee Collins. His pianist wore an orthopedic brace on his left hand, which had been damaged by a bullet. The drummer, "Pork Chops," sported the first Afro I ever saw. It seemed like he was always smoking a stick of "tea" – later known as "pot" – as he beat the drums.

The Victory Club offered a constantly changing program with never a dull moment. Among the regulars: a man who carried a chicken on his shoulders which he would set on the ground and talk to; a tall, thin fellow dressed in a blue Civil War frock coat that reached his ankles and was decorated with an assortment of medals and political buttons, who tried to play tunes (which he never got right) on a clarinet. Trumpeter Collins' hours were long, so he encouraged anyone and everyone to sit in. Once when Hugh, Bob, and I were partaking of a jam session with about a dozen or more players, a tipsy lady, no longer in the first blush of youth but not without viable assets, joined in by removing her clothing piece by piece. Need I add that the band played on, and on, until she even kicked off her shoes. The tune was the "St. Louis Blues."

Spring of 1949 found Hugh and me sharing a pad in Evanston, just north of Chicago. I can't recall why we moved up there. Evanston was the headquarters of the WCTU (Women's Christian Temperance Union), which meant it was "dry." No bars, no liquor stores, not much fun. Hugh finagled me a job at Hoos' Drug Store, next to Northwestern University. I worked as a counterman assembling lunch specials, making ice cream sodas, mopping floors, and admiring the female clerk's curvaceous figure which appeared to threaten the integrity of her uniform's buttons.

One spring day while I was preparing the eighty-cent lunch special – franks and beans and a slice of toast – a voice hailed me, using my boarding school nickname, "Beefie."[1] I looked up to see the Wisconsin rich kid who blew up toilets. He wanted to know what I was doing so far from home. I told him that my pal, Hugh, and I wanted to see the world, but after making it this far, we had to stop in order to earn enough money to carry on.

1 An item in *Time Magazine* had called my father "Beefie George Grosz." Pop was not fat. He checked his weight daily; he was "compact."

That evening my friend proposed that Hugh and I accompany him to an island owned by his family in a lake in upper Wisconsin. *What the hell, why not?* I thought. It couldn't be any worse in the woods than it was in the crummy dumps we'd been sharing in Chicago.

On the way we stopped for a week at his home, a mansion near the family factories. His mother, a feisty little lady, was a champion women's pistol shot. She practiced at a pistol range in the basement. Among the magazines lying about were publications by former FBI agents, warning of an imminent takeover of the U.S. Government by communist agents, harbingers of a creeping red infiltration of the United States by Russian sympathizers. In a few years the alcoholic Wisconsin Senator Joe McCarthy would attempt to build a political movement on the supposed Red Scare, only to be exposed as a xenophobic, power-hungry schemer and to sink into disrepute.

After racing round one evening with my drunk friend driving a car full of drunken college kids – not my favorite thing to do – we were stopped by a policeman who asked to see my friend's license, explaining that he was driving over the speed limit and appeared to be intoxicated. Whereupon he asked the officer, "Do you know who I am?" The officer glanced at the license and handed it back, saying, "Ok, Sir, just take it easy." Hugh and I looked at one another. If that had been one of us, we would have spent the night in the lockup and would have had to answer to a magistrate, followed by two weeks in the county jail.

But I had accepted the offer to go "clean up the summer house" on the family island. We went, and it was just two weeks of silly teenage hi-jinks: getting drunk, rolling in sand with silly girls, ramming one another's outboard motor boats.

When I got back to Chicago, I decided that it was time to go home. I had proven my proposition that I could support myself and do my own thing, whatever that might be.

Mom and Pop, brother Pete, and his fiancée, Lilian, met me at LaGuardia Airport. Soon I was back playing music for little money and working at low-wage day jobs, several months at a large nursery: dumb work, but healthy. Hugh came out from the city and he and my cousin Andreas, who had fought in the German army against the Russians during the last stand defending Berlin, worked at preparing a training track for race horses.

CHAPTER 10

Pfc. Grosz

In 1951, I made my debut on records: two 78 rpm discs. My clarinet pal, Frank Chace, came east to play clarinet. Hugh played cornet. John Dengler, a multi-instrumentalist, played baritone sax. Pianist Dick Wellstood brought along "Pops" Foster, who had spent many years with Louis Armstrong, to play bass; and Tommy Benford, who had recorded with Jelly Roll Morton, on drums.

In an effort to demonstrate that I had the potential to do more than plunk a guitar in a saloon or a dance hall, I enrolled in the School of General Studies at Columbia University. I had a room in Morningside Heights and went all over listening to jazz and playing wherever I could sit in, or wherever I could earn a few bucks.

My pal John Dengler, who played all the saxes as well as trumpet, trombone, tuba, and a smattering of piano, hired me to play a summer job in Pennsylvania's Pocono Mountain resort area, after which I returned to New York City, Columbia, and weekends playing at a Bronx bar called the Rathskeller.

The Korean War was going full tilt. In November of 1951, I passed the physical exam and without a chance to gather some belongings was whisked off to New Jersey, eventually landing at Fort Dix. There I spent four months undergoing basic training in tundra conditions, after which our company was shipped to Europe.

Our troopship bounced across the growling North Atlantic, plunging through waves. Most of my comrades spent the week-long journey seasick. The mess hall was deserted. I was lucky to be one of the few happy ocean crossers. I had crossed three times before; the ship's rocking didn't affect me as I ate solitary breakfasts with salt and pepper shakers sliding up and down the long mess hall tables.

I had brought my guitar along, which proved to be my passport to "soft" duty. Each night a handful of G.I.s who could play music and had brought their instruments got together and played on the upper deck for the entertainment of the officers and nurses on board. The captain in charge of entertainment saw to it that we enjoyed the privileges of the bar. So, while our chums were groaning and puking down below, we were playing and partying above.

After more than a week's journey, our troopship docked at Bremerhaven, Germany, and we were loaded onto a train that carried us from the North Sea to the town of Sonthofen in the southernmost part of the country. There we were housed in handsome, roomy stone buildings built for SS officer candidates.

We slept in well-appointed stone rooms that had housed elite Nazi trainees and ate in a spacious dining hall with a three-story-high window that gave a view of the German Alps – a view no doubt intended to inspire young SS officer candidates and to fill them with awe and heroic visions of their futures as establishers and perfectors of the Thousand-Year Reich to come.

The American occupiers of the defeated Deutschland had a clever way of defusing the nostalgia that some still harbored for dreams of Nazi grandeur. American authorities erased the glory of such Nazi shrines as the *Bürgerbräukeller* in Munich where Hitler's unsuccessful 1923 Putsch had originated, by turning it into an American Service Club. The jail where Hitler was sent as punishment for his role in the Putsch was at the town of Landsberg am Lech, southwest of Munich. It was here that Hitler wrote his manifesto, *Mein Kampf*. During the Nazi years, it was considered a shrine and was a place that Germans visited to pay homage to their Führer. After World War II, it was commandeered by the United States Army who named it War Criminal Prison No. I and used it to house important Nazis who escaped death sentences. It was to this old institution that I was assigned.

Soft duty. No running around in maneuvers, no sleeping in barracks, no cleaning of cannons and tanks. It was more like a nine-to-five job. Polish D.P.s, displaced persons who were left behind in Germany at war's end, served as para-militaries manning the watchtowers, guarding the prisoners, running the motor pool, etc. A handful of officers supervised. The bulk of the prisoners were middle-aged and not about to try to escape over the walls. Most of them had been officers who now worked in the carpenter's shop, the tailor shop, the shoe shop, the book bindery, etc. American Army officers were frequent visitors at the prison, stopping by to be measured for boots and uniforms which cost them a pittance. Sepp Dietrich, Hitler's chauffeur in the 1920s who ended up commanding an armored division, bound a book for me.

My first job at the prison was to work the night shift. The old building was cross-shaped, with three tiers of cells. On the ground floor in the center of the cross was a control booth from which a guard could observe the cells. This was manned twenty-four hours a day by American soldiers who kept an eye on the inmates, controlled their passes, and took headcounts each morning and evening.

When I first took headcounts of the various groups of inmates – former field marshals, generals, enlisted men, and even a few civilians) – I couldn't help but wonder what these august war criminals must be thinking as they stood lined up in their baggy prison trousers. A 22-year-old who had never seen conflict, I was being stared at by several full generals, a colonel who had escaped from burning tanks more than a dozen times, and Erhard Milch, the man who ran the Luftwaffe. While Hermann Göring had strutted about waving his field marshal's baton, it was Milch who kept the Luftwaffe's planes in the air. Another of the inmates had been Hitler's personal chauffeur in the twenties. By the end of the war he had been given command of his own Panzer (armored) division. That list aside, the majority of inmates had been rank-and-file soldiers who had violated the rules of war.

After a few weeks of cellblock duty, I was transferred to the postal section, where three of us bilingual G.I.s censored incoming and outgoing mail. Inmates were allowed to receive small parcels. In addition to my duties as a snooper, I was given the job of unit mail clerk, which entailed a daily run by jeep to the U.S. airbase about five miles away. There I picked up official and personal U.S. mail, then stopped at the Landsberg Post Office to get German mail and packages for the inmates.

For us military personnel, the prison work was almost like a nine-to-five civilian occupation. U.S. Army regulations stipulated that G.I.s who were not provided with recreational facilities – a beer hall, movie theater, PX, and other amenities – would be given a permanent pass which allowed them to find recreation off-post in civilian establishments, seven nights a week.

Landsberg had been a military town during the first and second World Wars. It was well equipped to help G.I.s spend their pay, boasting a movie theater, several hotels, a number of bars, and an ample supply of concupiscent "ladies" eager to take soldiers' minds off their all-male work environment.

If I hustled on my daily jeep run, I had just enough time for a cold beer to slake my hangover thirst at Robert's, a *gasthaus* (bar) on the edge of the woods. Often, I would notice another jeep or an Air Force truck parked there, being unloaded by G.I. personnel.

Robert, the proprietor, stood by checking off items being delivered: several dozen jerry cans of gasoline, winter Air Force parkas, cartons of cigarettes, cans of motor oil, etc., all black-market goods. Of course, I was aware that wherever heaps of governmental supplies are used and stored, there will be thievery. But this struck me as rather blatant. When I mentioned it to the older professional soldiers, they just chortled, remarking,

"What else is new?" When air patrolmen and German *Polizei* raided Robert's, all they found was a pack of Lucky Strikes in his mailbox.

When I got leave, I visited my Aunt Lotte and her husband, Onkel Otz, in Berlin. The train trip went through French, Russian, and American zones, so there were several stops when French, Russian, and American military police examined passports and trip orders. The French officers looked elegant in their sky-blue uniforms; the stubby Russian officers looked silly in their jodhpurs which only look smart when worn by tall persons.

Berlin was still largely in ruins. It had been pounded to a pulp; many sections were merely piles of rubble. I remember one five-story building of which only one wall remained standing – attached to which, at the fourth floor, was a level bathtub connected to the wall by a pipe.

When I returned from leave, I was moved to the prison's head office, where I served as a bilingual secretary and telephone operator. Our small detachment of about twenty-five soldiers and five or six officers functioned as supervisors. Now and then they would call for a cell check, when G.I.s and Polish guards poked about in inmates' possessions.

At *Fasching* (carnival) an Air Force captain and I, a Pfc., were assigned to be members of the *Elverrat*, the council of eleven who wear capes and "Punch and Judy" caps and function as honorees. For two weeks I was relieved of duty, and the captain and I had to represent the U.S. military. We of the council attended affairs hosted by Landsberg's mayor, stuffed ourselves at banquets, and attended dances whose music was provided by polka bands. I was glad when it was over, and I could get back to handling affairs at the prison office.

Sometimes I was the only G.I. running affairs. The colonel in charge had little to do; he was a National Guard officer logging in time for his retirement stipend. The prison ran itself; the other five officers were at home with their families, out fishing, or whatever. Whenever I'd get word that an important person was on his way to try on a uniform he had ordered from the prison tailor shop, or a pair of boots, or a newly bound book, I would get on the phone to summon an officer to meet the important visitor. Having a Pfc. greet a visiting brigadier general just wouldn't do.

Marty, the Chicago years

CHAPTER 11

Egghead Days

In 1953, my tour ended. I was home in Huntington just three days when a high school pal, Dick, rang me from Chicago. Dick, the loser, had married into one of Huntington's wealthy families. He and his bride had rented an apartment in Hyde Park and he was enrolled at the University of Chicago. Why didn't I come out and visit them? Okay, I did.

I wasn't there for more than two weeks when, lo and behold, Dick got a draft notice. The Korean War was still going full blast and the government wanted bodies; the couple sped back to Huntington. I got a little bachelor's pad and decided to try my luck as a student at the University of Chicago.

I had heard good things about U of C. Chancellor Hutchins had instituted a Great Books program at the school. Students had to read the original sources instead of merely reading about important historical texts. The University had no fraternities and had eliminated its "jock" culture by withdrawing from participation in intercollegiate sports. This suited me fine. As far as I was concerned, staying in shape made sense, but focusing huge sums of money and hours of practice on football so that young men could bash into one another, breaking bones and suffering concussions was, if not exactly criminal, a useless waste of time and energy.

The University of Chicago was termed an "egghead" school by students from state colleges and by many Chicagoans. That might have been true. I had difficulty fitting in with many of the students who were bright teenagers, quick to learn, and eager to study. I was 24, an experienced night owl, and a dedicated consumer of ardent spirits. It wasn't long before I was sharing my bed with a cafe-au-lait nurse, renewing relations with musicians, and picking up a music job here and there.

One morning about four months into my academic career, I was spending two hours rolling metal balls down a wooden inclined plane, stopwatch in hand, noting the slightest variations in the time it took the balls to reach the bumper at the bottom of the track. I understood the teacher's point: do not assume that just because things look the same, they are the same. In physics, the slightest variations can be extremely important. But two hours of rolling ball bearings with teenagers wasn't vanquishing my hangover. When class ended, I hastened to the Woodlawn Tap for a cold beer and a shot of bar whiskey. My college career was over.

No college meant no G.I. Bill. Ergo: no money. I started reading the want ads and hitting on friends, and before long I landed a job as a copywriter for the catalog of a mail-order company named Spiegel's. Because of its central location, Chicago was the mail-order capital of the U.S. I wrote about shoes, work clothing, parkas; in other words, men's clothing.

There were about a dozen of us copywriters. None of them wanted to write the drivel that was sandwiched between photos of boots "with night-glow welts," long johns, overalls, all-weather overcoats, and work gloves "built to take it." I earned enough to pay for my basement pad and to buy a couple of beers to accompany a dinner of Polish sausage and sauerkraut cooked on my four-burner stove.

I spent a lot of evenings practicing guitar, not just to improve, but also to be in shape when someone called me to play jazz. After two thirds of a year spent fashioning catalog trash, I got a call from my pal Frank Chace. He was playing five nights a week in a trio at a club on Rush Street, Chicago's nightlife strip. The group consisted of piano, banjo, and clarinet.

The venue was the brainchild of an advertising agency proprietor named Burton Browne. At that time (the early 1950s), Illinois had a state law which mandated that liquor sold at bars had to be paid for in cash. Wholesale liquor merchants and private clubs (i.e. university clubs, golf clubs, etc.) could accept checks or just signatures. Chicago in those years was a busy convention center. All year long, manufacturers put on lavish events at the Merchandise Mart, the biggest building of its kind in the world; at hotels; and at theaters. Ergo, downtown was filled with throngs of buyers and sellers looking for a good time and to cement deals, preferably at a bar with entertainment and sexy waitresses.

Nothing new there, but how were the visiting tractor salesmen supposed to pay for all the drinks they bought to jolly their potential customers? Should they carry strong boxes filled with cash secured to their bodies with chains? Burton Browne sat down with his lawyers and had a brainstorm. He'd start a *private* club on Rush Street. For five dollars a head, strangers could become members. If their I.D.s checked out, they could charge drinks and tips. At the end of the month, they'd receive their bills in the mail. The idea caught on.

CHAPTER 12

Gaslight Club

The original Gaslight Club had four large rooms, each with a bar and a piano. The motif was a mixture of Gay Nineties and Roaring Twenties. The piano players and bartenders wore multicolored striped shirts, sleeve garters, and vests, and some wore derbies.

My pal Frank and the banjo player wore similar shirts and bow ties. The pianist was short. He wore a dark blue frock coat with a stand-up collar and badge, à la the Keystone Kops.

The banjo player was leaving, so Frank called me to take his place. Even though I didn't own a banjo, I leapt at the offer. Bye, bye day job. I bought a cheap instrument, was measured for a shirt, and became a banjo player.

The club was popular. Pianos were plunking. Waitresses dressed in scanty costumes, fairly tame by today's standards, hustled drinks.

The room where we worked was called the Speakeasy.

Marty, Gaslight Club, 1950s

Customers entered it through a telephone booth. When seated, they were handed little wooden sticks with a wooden ball at one end. The jolly patrons were encouraged to beat time with our music. The result: a cacophonous mess.[1]

The leader of our trio, Jess, was in his 60s. He had played piano all over the Midwest in theater pit bands, restaurants and bars, radio studios, and on a program devoted to selling various makes of used but reconditioned pianos called "Warehouse 39," upon which he would play selections in order to demonstrate their tone, resonance, and easy action. When I asked Jess which make of piano – there were many back then – he liked best, he replied that he liked all of them. Because there was only one piano in the studio upon which he demonstrated: a Steinway. *Caveat Emptor.*

The atmosphere created by waitresses who sang, patrons who banged on tables and often bellowed the songs of their frat-house days – "The Sheik of Araby (With No Pants On)," "Margie," "Nothing Could Be Finer than to Be in Carolina," "Alexander's Ragtime Band," "Yes Sir, That's My Baby," "The St. Louis Blues," "My Blue Heaven," "Peg O'My Heart," "Sweet Georgia Brown" – and on and on, induced thirst among the jolly patrons and, not the least, among our trio.

While I was toiling at the Gaslight Club, I married an intelligent lady, Rachel Whelan, valedictorian of her class at George Rogers Clark High School in Whiting, Indiana, home to a giant Standard Oil refinery that bordered South Chicago. Her

---

1   After seventy years as a professional musician (I joined the Musician's Union, AF of M, in 1948), I am convinced that most people can't carry a tune, nor can they keep time.

parents had come from a small town in Indiana, bringing their narrow-minded rural ways with them. Rachel had been offered a scholarship to the University of Chicago which her mother would not allow her to accept, afraid that her daughter would become a liberal intellectual – which is exactly what happened anyway.

Rachel eventually became the head secretary of Chicago University's humanities department and would earn a master's degree in English literature, play clarinet in an informal university orchestra, and manage our household finances. She worked days and I worked nights, wherefore I cooked the family's suppers, an arrangement that worked out for the best. Our two sons attended local schools, to which they walked. I was teaching myself to read music, and to write it, so I could fashion arrangements for recordings.

CHAPTER 13

Eddie Condon

One day in 1956, I got a call from Johnny Windhurst, a talented trumpeter who played at Eddie Condon's jazz club in lower Manhattan. Eddie and Johnny were in Chicago for the wedding of the daughter of one of Eddie's oldest friends and supporters, "Squirrel" Ashcraft, a lawyer who had lived in the suburbs of Chicago but was then settled in Princeton, New Jersey.

Eddie was born in Goodland, Indiana, in the early years of the century, the youngest child of a large family that hailed from County Mayo, Ireland.

He reminded me of a leprechaun, quick-witted with a gift of gab. His father had run a saloon in Goodland, but with the onset of prohibition he relocated to South Chicago where he became a policeman.

As a teenager, Eddie taught himself banjo. Possessed of an unusually keen ear, he was soon touring with a band, advertised as a youthful banjo sensation. It wasn't long before he established himself in Chicago, then (in the 1920s) the jazz capital of the world. Many New Orleans musicians, black and white, had relocated to the Windy City, including Louis Armstrong, Jelly Roll Morton, the Dodds Brothers, the New Orleans Rhythm Kings, Jimmie Noone, etc. The magical Bix Beiderbecke was an important presence in the Chicago scene, although he hailed from Davenport, Iowa.

In the late 1920s, hot musicians were in demand in New York. Eddie, Benny Goodman, saxist Bud Freeman, pianists Joe Sullivan and Jess Stacy, drummers Gene Krupa, Dave Tough, and George Wettling all relocated to New York.

While prohibition lasted Eddie was living well, playing with a hot combination called the Mound City Blue Blowers which was popular with the society crowd. After repeal, Eddie played in combos on 52nd Street, with the outstanding trumpeters Bunny Berigan and Red Allen.

As the 1930s rolled on, Eddie was regarded as one of the first rhythm guitarists in jazz. Clarinetist Artie Shaw summed it up when he remarked that Eddie had a beat that would make a mummy keep time. Eddie's sharp-tongued wit was often quoted, especially when a pedantic French jazz critic, Hugues Panassié, arrived in New York 1939 and began to spout dictums about American jazz. Eddie's riposte, "Do I go over to France and tell them how to jump on a grape?" was much quoted.

I wasn't working, so I grabbed a train for the Loop and walked over to Eddie's hotel. He was sharing a room with Johnny, who met me at the door. Eddie was in the bathroom squeezing his grog blossoms, after which he employed pancake makeup to conceal the damage (need I add that Eddie was a world-class drinker).

To prepare himself, Eddie rolled six sticks of "tea" which he placed in his watch pocket. His plan was to drop by the Blue Note jazz club to say hello to its owner, Frank Holzfeind. It was a large place, fairly well attended, with some musicians playing whose names I've forgotten. It wasn't long before Eddie was recognized and asked to join a table full of well-heeled customers. Eddie was a world-class schmoozer. John and I audited the music.

I had set myself a little task: before the night was through, I would get the poker-faced "I tell the funny stories" Condon to crack up. I hadn't a clue how to accomplish this task, but I was sure I would come up with something.

The night rolled on, and at closing time the Blue Note boss joined the three of us in search of sustenance. In those days there was a 24-hour eatery called Ricketts on the Near North Side. We went and ordered drinks and hamburgers. *How am I going to get this guy Condon to laugh?* I thought. My first attempt was a failure: a filthy joke which I told with admirable attention to detail and vivid language. Eddie nodded as if to indicate that he appreciated my skill.

The night oozed on, and then Eddie remembered that his drinking buddy Johnny Mercer's musical, *Li'l Abner*, had opened on Broadway. Windhurst was dispatched to a nearby 24-hour newsstand to find a copy of *Variety*, the showbiz paper that would have a review.

The paper was laid on our table for Eddie to peruse. Alas, he was too vain to be seen wearing glasses. The paper was passed to Windhurst who also excused himself, saying his eyes were too blurry from booze, as did club owner Holzfeind. This left me. I had consumed my share of *spiritus fermenti*, but I felt I could still assemble letters of the alphabet to spell words. I cleared my throat, grasped the paper, and launched into my version of the review. It went something like this:

> Li'l Abner, *the new Johnny Mercer-Gene de Paul musical about the goings-on at Dogpatch, cartoonist Al Capp's hillbilly heaven, was ushered in by strong performances from Brad Smelter (made-up name) as Abner and Rosemary Bump (made-up name), the beautiful rustic who vainly pursues him. Smelter, despite suffering from a painful dose of the clap, sang and acted with gusto. Bump pursued him across the stage, at one time having to halt as one of her strategic costume zippers lost its grasp.*
>
> *Pappy and Mammy Yokum, Abner's parents, were played by Herbert Hoover and Kate Smith, both of whom capered from the wings dressed in gunny sacks and swinging jugs of moonshine, etc., etc.*

By this time, I had poker-faced Condon and the others cracking up, chortling, and even venturing a guffaw or two. Mission accomplished.

CHAPTER 14

Chet Baker

It was in the 1960s that I first saw Chet Baker, the gifted California trumpet player-singer. He had been booked into a mob-owned Chicago nightclub called the Nob Hill where he was appearing with his pianist, bassist, and drummer. The evening that I went to hear Baker, attendance was light. As I took a seat at the bar, Baker was cuddling a microphone, whisper-singing one of his signature songs, "My Funny Valentine," a maudlin 1930s ballad by Rodgers & Hart that he had resuscitated. He resembled a cherubic Jack Palance. In an era when nightclub entertainers wore tuxedos or dark suits, Chet was attired in an open-collared green shirt, tan trousers, and striped socks – prompting one customer to ask the bartender, "Who's the fruitcake in the sandals?"

Chet was backed up by his own pianist, bassist, and drummer, three zombies who appeared to be mesmerized. Could it be, I mused, that Baker and his cronies were under the influence of a controlled substance?

In the ensuing years, Baker's dependence on drugs would become more obvious as his behavior grew more bizarre. Obviously, things were not going well for this gifted man. In the grip of an addiction that he could not escape, his unhappy life would deteriorate.

Years later I happened to be in Amsterdam when newspaper headlines proclaimed his death in that city. He had exited his third-floor hotel room window. Was it his choice? We'll never know.

CHAPTER 15

The Village Stompers:
Road Version

Three years into my stint at the Gaslight Club, I was becoming punch drunk from banging a banjo for garrulous, intoxicated salesmen and conventioneers. So, when an old New York pal asked me to join a road trip of a group he worked with, I accepted. The band, called the Village Stompers, would start in the New York area and travel across the country, ending up in Los Angeles.

A group of New York City studio musicians had recorded an album of tunes in a style that was dubbed "folk-dixie," which I thought was a sleazy "pop" concept. It attempted to combine commercial folk music and traditional (Dixieland) jazz. When I heard the album, it became obvious to me that the concoction served neither idiom well. However, I wanted to travel west and find out if there was work for me out there. So I bit the bullet, flew to New York City, and joined a group of players who would more or less imitate the numbers on the LP.

Their big hit recording was "Washington Square." It started with an amplified guitar vamp over which I plunked out the melody on banjo. After one chorus, a trombone *gliss* brought in trumpet and clarinet, and a jammed ensemble followed. This was the group's "hit" formula that was later applied to other tunes, such as "Follow the Drinking Gourd" and Roger Miller's "King of the Road."

The band's leader played trumpet, didn't swing, and made corny announcements that he got out of a handbook that purportedly provided bandleaders with humorous zingers such as, "Here's a number that was a hit for 'Peter, Paul and Mounds,' oops I mean 'Mary.'"

The band had a two-week engagement in Lake Tahoe, which boasted a block of gambling casinos. We played two shows a night. One night during the break I was killing time at the 10-cent slots – a potential jackpot winner has to start somewhere – when I heard a commotion at our casino entrance. I went over to see what was going on. A blonde lady, dressed in a white gown and dragging a mink stole behind her, was coming into the casino quite unsteadily. She was followed by a tall, tanned, dark-haired fellow in a sharkskin suit. As she entered the casino, she addressed the man saying, "Look, you big piece of shit."

"Hey baby, you got it wrong," he replied.

To which she retorted, snarling, "Take your 'Hey baby' and shove it up your ass."

I could go on, but you get the idea.

What's happening? I thought. Then as she staggered closer, I recognized her face. It belonged to June Allyson, Miss Wholesome, sweetheart of countless films in which she played the girl next door, promising to wait forever 'til young Mr. Wholesome would return from his stint in the Air Force dropping bombs on Tokyo. Miss Allyson had a knack for making her face look devoted without a hint of lewdness, and here she was letting it all hang out. It was pleasing to learn that what one suspected went on in the corridors of power, be it Washington, New York, or Hollywood, really went on. After all, it goes on everywhere else.

We rolled into Los Angeles for an appearance at a large supper club called the Crescendo. Three of us found accommodation at a seedy old hotel that summoned up visions of the 1920s. In the lobby stood a grand piano covered with a large cloth sheet known as a piano scarf. In the elevator I encountered gentlemen with dyed hair, comb-overs, a touch of rouge on the cheeks and dyed pencil-thin mustaches, wearing pleated jackets that were stylish in the '30s. Once an elderly lady's handbag popped open, causing a pint bottle of Old Overholt to fall to the floor with a clank. I picked it up and handed it to her and was rewarded with a sweet smile.

We played at the Crescendo on Sunset Strip as part of a nightly show that featured the appearance of Vaughn Meader, a comedian who had sold thousands of records and made loads of television appearances lampooning President John F. Kennedy, Jackie Kennedy, and their family. After Kennedy's assassination, the record was taken off the shelves, Meader's appearances were cancelled, and he vanished from the public eye.

This engagement was to mark his comeback. Opening night was packed with celebrities and reporters. Another comedian opened the show, then came a fellow who held a pistol-grip microphone and imitated sounds of a duck-hunt, horses crossing a stream, and different model car doors slamming. Meader had worked hard developing new material, but it couldn't match up to his previous work. Somewhere in this show we rendered "Washington Square" and a tune or two.

For two weeks the nightly attendance dwindled, and then we hit the road back to New York. I left the band at Chicago and showed up at home with a few bucks and a bag of dirty clothes, delighted to be back with Rachel and the kids.

CHAPTER 16

Gaslight to Velvet Swing

After the Village Stompers road trip, I jobbed around Chicago playing jobs that were mostly mundane but paid the rent. Henry, a tuba player, hired me to work all types of silly gigs: the opening of a Wisconsin cheese store in Union Station, an all-day job (tuba, banjo, trumpet) for the Riverside Savings Bank for which we had to wear propeller beanies and play "Down by the Riverside" over and over.

I completed a trio at the Gaslight Club, which had moved to a two-story 1880s house with a wide winding stairway to the second floor. Our pianist, Art Gronwall, had some '20s jazz credits and was an improvement. The new leader, Freddie, played trumpet and clarinet. He could render any piece of music at sight, transpose, and double on alto, tenor, and baritone saxophone.

Television and radio stations had discovered that they didn't need live music like ours anymore; pre-recorded tapes could do just as well for their purposes and save the broadcasters a pile of money. Hence musicians who had earned tidy incomes were getting laid off.

Later, Freddie got an offer to play at a club in St. Paul owned by the maker of Pearson's Chocolate-Covered Mints for the summer. I took my wife and son along. We stayed in a roomy old Victorian home in Dinkytown – the town's actual name – where students and teachers at the University of Minnesota lived. A local pianist completed the trio.

At summer's end, I was back in Chicago and back at the Gaslight Club. This time the trio was under the leadership of an entertainer-pianist who did all sorts of cheesy piano stunts, like striking the keys with his palms turned upward and turning around on his piano stool and playing with his hands behind his back.

He was something of an entertainer, but with scant knowledge of jazz. To me, his best suite was his supply of "put downs," some of which I still remember. When the drunks grew raucous and yelled for stupid tunes, which was most of the time, and a polite rejoinder such as "We just played that on our last set," wouldn't cause the pest to stop demonstrating, Frankie would say, "Sir, do I go where you work and kick the shovel out of your hands?" And if that didn't silence the pest, Frankie would press on, often ending with, "Sir, I'd ask you to keep your mouth shut, but I don't want to ruin your sex life." This usually got a roar from the other patrons and vanquished the pest. A Chicago police detective and an automobile-repossessor were ever-present, moonlighting to control the drunks.

After a while I was able to get my pal Murph, a superior

trumpet player, on the job. Murph had all the ingredients that should have guaranteed him a place amongst the top musicians. He had played in drummer Gene Krupa's orchestra before he was drafted in World War II. After that, he played with Jimmy Dorsey, for ice shows, and with any number of small groups in jazz clubs. Starting in the '20s as a drummer in Pottstown, Pennsylvania, he had jobbed with several local bands and stunned his bandmates late one night by picking up a trumpet and rendering a solo on "Stardust."

In the Krupa Orchestra, he played alongside his idol Roy Eldridge in the trumpet section. Murph possessed all the right ingredients: tone, time, pitch, and lots of ideas.

The Gaslight Club was wearing us down. We played the same tunes over and over. Frankie's ponderous, blacksmith touch on the keyboard and his roller-coaster sense of tempo were wearying me.

Murph was the first to go: too many absences as he began losing his battle with the bottle. Another trumpet player took over. He was sober, took care of business, and laid off the sauce. Okay, but uninspiring. In fact, boring. I got an offer from a bar called the Velvet Swing for more money than I was earning, so I took it.

When one entered the Velvet Swing, one saw a bar over which a scantily-dressed "lady" arched back and forth on a swing. The bar opened upon a back room where a four-piece combo tooted at patrons seated at tables. An aging flapper would sing with them.

I handled intermissions by playing twenties tunes on the banjo: "Ain't She Sweet," "Sweet Sue," "Peg o'My Heart," "JaDa," winding up with an up-tempo killer-diller like "The World is

Waiting for the Sunrise." To add variety to my act, I began to sing and indulge in verbal clowning.

Many of the lines I tossed off were ancient, but worked, such as when a drunken patron got up from his table, knocking his chair over and grabbing the tabletop for balance and upsetting glasses as he staggered toward the men's room. I would grab the microphone and ask, "Sir, is that how you always walk, or are you wearing your wife's underwear?" A sure-fire laugh-getter.

While plying my schlocky act at the Velvet Swing, a Canadian entrepreneur offered me a job at the brand-new "Beverly Hills" Motor Hotel about ten miles north of Toronto. I would do my banjo act at supper theater that was part of the motel. The pay was right, so I accepted, suggesting that he hire some of my pals to comprise a combo that would play for the acts and for dancing. He agreed, and off we went to Toronto.

CHAPTER 17

Toronto

The stage show at the Beverly Hills Motor Hotel consisted of a girl singer trying to make a name for herself, a foul-mouthed old harridan who was funny but whose language was more fitting for a strip club, and me and my banjo. The combo, which included several of my musical buddies, accompanied the acts and then played for dancing. Fox-trots, rhumbas, and waltzes were still popular.

I had been yearning to play less banjo and more guitar. Over the preceding years I had developed my own guitar tuning, which consisted of retaining banjo tuning in thirds on the top three strings, and tuning the bottom three strings in fifths, similar to cello tuning. The result permitted me to play in "stride" piano style which I loved, but also allowed me to play rhythm in the regular 4/4 style favored by swing-band guitarists.

The Beverly Hills Motel manager lodged us, the six-piece combo and me, in another motel about ten miles away. Our motel advertised hourly rates, which meant that each room functioned as a 24-hour Cupid's bower. Day and night the motel resounded with a gallimaufry of auditory groans, squeaks, squeals, and thumps that began to get on my nerves.

One day John, our trumpet player, came by my ground-floor room to pick me up for lunch. He was one of two musicians in our troupe who had a car. It was noon, and I was finishing dressing, when we heard a car pull up, the door in the next room being opened, and a man and woman laughing.

The cinderblock wall between my room and the adjoining one had a six-inch gap at the floor level through which phone lines had been run. John kneeled and peered into the adjoining room, motioning for me to take a peek. All I could see was a woman's hand rolling her nylon stockings down, and a man's brogans thumping to the floor. I could hear the woman complimenting her assignator's physique, whereupon he burst into the song "More" in a rich baritone voice.

That did it. I grabbed my guitar, beckoned John to join me, and we both sang "More" as loudly as we could.

Five minutes later their door slammed, and they roared off in a big Buick.

The next day the manager, an English grandmother, invited me into her apartment for tea and scones. She told me that one of the two second-story rooms above the motel office was available. It took me fifteen minutes to move in. Sleep at last.

On our days off, some of us would drive down to Toronto. I particularly wanted to catch pianist Don Ewell, who was performing at a club called the Golden Nugget on Yonge Street with Henry Cuesta, a clarinetist. Both had spent the previous two years touring with trombonist Jack Teagarden's combo. I had recorded with Don. During the two months that I worked in Canada, Henry Cuesta and I got to know each other, which resulted in my working numerous times in Toronto, either with Henry's combo or as a single. I was playing more guitar and less banjo.

CHAPTER 18

Wit's End

Back in Chicago, the jazz situation was bleak. Steady jobs were disappearing. Night clubs weren't hiring as many name acts as before. My trumpeter pal Murph and I had a trio job in Waukegan which was north of the city, a long haul back and forth – especially the drive home, fighting to keep my eyes open. To get work, I even bought an amplifier. I detested amps, but in order to survive the disheartening jobs, one had to be loud. So, I played for weddings, birthday parties, and "industrials."

Industrials were what bookers called engagements for conventions. The bands would play peppy tunes as the conventioneers filed into a motel ballroom for dinner, after which CEOs would make long-winded speeches, after which other executives would make more long-winded speeches. Then would come awards to employees with the best sales records. The band leader would call the musicians to attention so that they could punctuate the presentations with appropriate music. For example, if the award recipient came from California, we would send him or her to the podium with as much of "California, Here I Come" as it took to accompany him or her to the podium. If the recipient was from New York, we'd play a bit of "Manhattan," and later "New York, New York"; if from Texas, "The Eyes of Texas," and so forth. Should the award winner come from a state to which we couldn't attach a song, like, say, Delaware, we'd play a bit of "Happy Days Are Here Again," or some other optimistic tune.

What had all this to do with jazz? Very little. By 1970, the pop music scene was undergoing the radical, relentless, and heartless changes that occur when the younger generation matures, and the next generation comes along. Only this time, the changes were more dramatic and more rapid.

For example, the Polka originated in Bohemia in the 1830s. It was still being danced to over one hundred years later. In the 1950s, Chicago and Milwaukee still had live Polka hours on television featuring full orchestras of about fifteen musicians. A children's hour, *Bozo's Circus*, had a circus band about the same size. Ten years later, these bands had been replaced by computer-generated sound tracks.

Weekly broadcasts of live symphonic music and operas had been heard on radio since the early 1930s; now they had also disappeared.

Fortunately, I was working in a quintet at the Blackstone Hotel five nights a week. While guests arrived, we played – what else? dinner music – after which we played dance tunes with a good bit of jazz thrown in.

Thus, the onset of the 1970s did not bode well for the jazz

business in Chicago. My comfortable job at the Blackstone Hotel came to an end. New owners decided that their property didn't need to present live music anymore. The era when a hotel or restaurant furnished a space for dancing had come to an end. The time when every restaurant and bar employed a piano player had passed. The directories of musician's unions in various cities were becoming thinner.

I found employment by playing jobs in Toronto until my connection, clarinetist Henry Cuesta, moved to California, where he became the last of several clarinet stars with the Lawrence Welk Orchestra. I took whatever work I could find. Since the heyday of the banjo was past, I bought an amp and began to play a succession of silly jobs: weddings, bar mitzvahs, political dinners, Las Vegas nights in church basements, early morning pep rallies for salesmen, retirement parties on excursion boats, even a funeral for which we had to pretend we were in New Orleans. The Crescent City burials had become hokey enough with ex-boppers pretending to sound as if they were their grandfathers.

My wife's job kept us above water, but I was becoming depressed.

Once in a while I worked with a Gaslight Club Road Show that played gigs in midwestern states. The troupe consisted of a six-piece band and four "girls" who thought they could dance. Whatever it was that the chorus lines of the '20s and '30s had, it eluded these hoofers.

The troupe worked on weekend nights in Illinois, Indiana, Iowa, Wisconsin, and Michigan, states that had "dry" counties or townships. It's difficult to imagine now, but bars in those locations either didn't exist or had to close so early that customers had more fun drinking at home. The exceptions were private clubs, which did a thriving business. I peddled corn in countless Elks and Rotary clubs where the jolly midwestern burghers drank themselves into oblivion.

These occasional employments notwithstanding, I was desperate to play "grown-up music" and to earn some steady money. I sent for a listing of available government jobs, and at Christmas I worked as a temp at the Chicago Post Office, at that time the largest in the United States.

I had to rise before my wife and two sons to find a place to park and report for work at 7 a.m., formerly my bedtime on many occasions. Believe it or not, I enjoyed driving downtown in the wee hours. The work wasn't demanding; I spent my days pushing gurneys filled with mail in and out of elevators and taking frequent coffee breaks with interesting fellow temps. The pay wasn't terrific, but it helped, and the work made me feel useful. When the Christmas season was over, I was back in the no-work doldrums.

These times of inactivity were occasionally relieved by a prestige job, like when I was asked to assemble a group of jazz veterans for a concert presented by the Chicago Historical Society. I got hold of veterans of the halcyon days of jazz in Chicago: the twenties.[1] After the first half of the concert, Gene Krupa, who

---

1   In the 1920s, the jazz capital moved from New Orleans to Chicago. Scores of New Orleans musicians moved to Chicago to play for dancers in ballrooms and bars. A partial listing of major influencers includes: cornetists King Oliver and Louis Armstrong; clarinetists Johnny Dodds, Jimmie Noone, and Leon Roppolo; trombonists Kid Ory and George Brunies; pianist Jelly Roll Morton; guitarists Bud Scott and Johnny St. Cyr; bassists Steve Brown and Wellman Braud; drummer Baby Dodds.

was appearing at the prominent jazz club the London House, took over the drums, propelling us to a rousing finale.

The tie-in with the historical theme created some work, largely for programs in schools. Jim Lanigan, who had played with the original Austin High musicians in the 1920s, provided historical authenticity while also demonstrating his superb technique. After graduation from high school, Jim had become a sought-after bass and tuba player, working in theater pit bands and winding up in the celebrated Chicago Symphony. He was eventually forced to leave the symphony because severe arthritis in his fingering hand prevented him from holding notes of long duration effectively. However, he could still use his bow for most purposes. For me, it was a treat to hear something else besides the endless, unvaried chains of quarter notes that jazz bassists were using, and still do.

While occasional concerts with jazz groups were musically rewarding, they didn't occur frequently enough to pay the bills. So, I kept searching for a way to bring in money.

Then there was Jazz at Noon. This was an event where every Friday, amateurs could bring instruments and sit in with one another, supported by a three-man rhythm section. The participants paid a modest fee which allowed them to partake of a buffet lunch and relive their youthful amateur jazz-musician

Having been steeped in the New Orleans sound, the following Chicago players would go on to attain fame: cornetists Muggsy Spanier, Bix Beiderbecke (an Iowan who played with Chicagoans), and Jimmy McPartland; clarinetists Frank Teschemacher, Benny Goodman, Joe Marsala, and Pee Wee Russell; trombonist Floyd O'Brien; saxophonist Bud Freeman; pianists Joe Sullivan and Jess Stacy; bassist and tuba player Jim Lanigan; drummers Dave Tough, George Wettling, and Gene Krupa; guitarists Eddie Condon, Jack Bland, and Dick McPartland.

days. The event also served to encourage interest in other jazz events, concerts, and dances.

The results of putting four or five middle-aged businessmen, who never were any great shakes, and none of whom gave evidence that they practiced their instruments, together, and expecting their efforts to produce coherent music were predictable. At best they sounded like feeding time at the zoo.

Riding home on the "L" after these sessions, which paid little and lowered my spirits, I would wonder what I could do. As I got off the train, I felt that the station should read "Wit's End." I was a 45-year-old guy who played guitar and banjo and didn't know any way to make a living except by strumming and adding a vocal to engage the audience.

CHAPTER 19

Soprano Summit

Then one afternoon in the early 1970s, as I was assembling an Irish stew in the kitchen – I enjoyed cooking; my wife didn't – the phone rang. It was a Bob Wilber from New York. Bob played clarinet and soprano saxophone and a few other instruments. I'd met him when I was a teenager just starting out. He had studied with the famous Sidney Bechet who had made the soprano sax a jazz instrument, and with legendary Harlem stride pianist Willie "The Lion" Smith. Bob was looking for a guitarist to work with his new quintet, Soprano Summit, featuring himself and Kenny Davern on soprano saxes and clarinets, along with a rhythm section of guitar, bass, and drums. Would I be interested in playing with the quintet? Would I!

"Bob, are you near a window?" I asked him.

"Yes, why?" he replied.

"Because if you look sharply you will notice a tiny dot. Look

Soprano Summit, 1975: Kenny Davern, soprano sax;
Marty Grosz, guitar; Connie Kay, drums; Bob Wilber, clarinet;
George Duvivier, bass

every day and you'll notice that tiny dot gradually growing larger and larger until one day, you'll look and it will be me."

So, I flew to New York, and lo and behold, before you could recite the Penal Code of the State of New Jersey, I was strumming my guitar and singing in Carnegie Hall with Soprano Summit.

The occasion was a concert presented by the New York Jazz Repertory Company which was run by George Wein, producer of the Newport Jazz Festivals. The concert was devoted to the music of the legendary Ferdinand "Jelly Roll" Morton, composer of "King Porter Stomp," which became a mega-hit for the Benny Goodman Orchestra; "Wolverine Blues," a staple of the jazz repertoire in the 1920s and 1930s; "Buddy Bolden's Blues"; and "Sweet Substitute."

Before Soprano Summit appeared on stage, I remember that my knees were trembling and my throat was dry, whereupon I sought to obtain courage from a pint of whiskey I had brought along to give me "Dutch courage." Carnegie Hall represented the "big time" to a saloon player like me. Carmen Mastren, a fine guitarist who had played with jazz combos and was a star of Tommy Dorsey's orchestra for which he had written arrangements, many of which became hits, was also on the concert program. He introduced himself, assuring me that I would do just fine. His words helped. In later years we would talk on the phone.

Soprano Summit's half of the concert went off without a hitch. Bob Wilber's arrangement of "Froggie Moore Rag" was applauded by the audience, not for rousing cacophony, but because it went from six men dishing out punchy sounds to four men drastically reducing the volume. The "trio," which is what the main part of a march or rag is called, was performed by a quartet of guitar (playing single-note lead) harmonized with two clarinets and acoustic string bass to form a quasi-barbershop quartet, while the piano and drums remained silent. The audience was surprised and applauded the effect.

After the statement of the trio, the drums and piano came back in, and the performance galloped to its conclusion. One of the pieces we swung into was "Milenberg Joys," a rousing stomp. On the eve of the concert, I was asked to sing this up-tempo number. I tried my best to memorize the words and had scribbled them on a shirt cardboard which I placed on my music stand. When it was time for the vocal, I put one leg up on my chair to rest my guitar on, strummed mightily, and bellowed, "Rock my soul with the Milenberg Joys." The audience, mostly thirty and over, gave me a hearty ovation, a few even rose out of their seats. *Is that all it takes?* I thought. I hadn't done anything different than I usually did when I sang a number. I wasn't any great shakes, but I did relieve the monotony of uninterrupted instrumental music.

I would experience this phenomenon again and again, especially at jazz parties.

CHAPTER 20

Jazz Parties

F rom the 1960s until the early years of the twenty-first century, jazz parties helped to keep the music going. These gatherings were organized and produced as a way for mostly middle-aged jazz fans to enjoy the music they had grown up with, which was being replaced by rock and roll. From modest beginnings of ten to fifteen participants they grew, until one jazz party in Denver presented forty or fifty players in all sorts of combinations.

For about a quarter of a century, jazz parties were fashionable. Most of the attendees had grown up in the '20s and '30s. For them, the music performed at these affairs recalled the songs of their youth when jazz was a byproduct of dance music. In those years, most musicians read music, often from workmanlike scores prepared by arrangers who stressed the melody of a tune. Occasionally, gifted players improvised ad lib solos on the dance

Marty with Joe Newman, trumpet; Bob Wilber, alto sax;
Bill Watrous, trombone, 1977

tunes, and now and then a particular player would be given space to improvise.

From its inception, jazz was music to dance to. In the early years of the twentieth century, it insinuated itself into dance music, replacing the Bunny Hug, the Grizzly Bear, Ragtime, and waltzes. Jazz bands played fox trots and one-steps in 2/4 or 4/4 time, in peppy rhythms that made it difficult for couples to press their bodies together on the dance floor. In the first half of the twentieth century, parents and politicians frowned upon hints of salacious conduct between the sexes, especially contact between bodies in public.

Even in the permissive atmosphere of New Orleans – known for its bordellos – it wasn't until the wee hours that musicians played slow tunes, which were often blues rendered with an assortment of instrumental growls and moans meant to suggest the sounds that accompanied mating.

Jam sessions took place after the dance band musicians were through for the night and were looking for a club where they could pick up women and unwind. Practically all clubs hired piano players or small combos, and when a "swing star" who was in town dropped by, he would be asked to sit in. Often several players would show up and be asked to play and match talents with local favorites. It didn't take long before accounts of those musical battles took on the qualities of myths: the favorite versions told of little-known local players "wasting" the reputations of the celebrated guest performers. While it is true that on occasion a little-known local player would astound name-band players, it was not the rule.

The well-organized jazz parties that popped up throughout the country and overseas in the 1950s until the beginning
of the twenty-first century were planned and advertised. Most
of the participating musicians were established practitioners
whose glory days were behind them. Patrons were given a detailed
schedule of events which consisted of 45-minute (sometimes
longer) sets with listings of the participants. Each set had a
three-piece rhythm section of piano, bass, and drums, and
sometimes guitar, though most guitarists were amplified and
did not strum rhythm.[1]

As a rule, the jazz parties, instead of delivering a music
empowered by fresh creative energy, a music replete with contrasts
and nuances, served up a manic stew of clichés performed by
musicians forced to perform with others with whom they shared
little common ground, whose styles did not match theirs.

There were a few exceptions: female vocalists whose intimate
styles obligated their accompanying musicians to dampen their
egos and play softly, or a rare solo piano set *sans* overbearing
drums and bass.

One of the largest jazz parties was staged first in Colorado
Springs and then moved to Denver by a champion self-promoter,
Dick Gibson.

Gibson was never loath to trumpet his "achievements,"
which included his participation in the last minstrel troupe in
America as a young man, during which his singing so impressed
a Mercury Records executive that he offered him a generous

---

1   I was one of the rare exceptions. The sound man stuck a mic in front of me
which I often pushed away. Rhythm guitar needs to blend with, not overwhelm,
the other rhythm instruments.

Jamming with Joe Venuti, 1976

Marty with Joe Venuti, 1977

contract. He claimed membership in the University of Alabama Crimson Tide football team in some capacity; he had studied writing with William Faulkner; he had known L. Ron Hubbard, the founder of Scientology, "when Hubbard was just a pimply-faced writer of science fiction," as he used to say. Listening to Dick Gibson's recital of his accomplishments, I got the impression that he must be over 100 years old to have been involved in so many varied enterprises.

His jazz parties, which were well-intentioned endeavors, grew from weekends featuring about a dozen musicians to four-day carnivals with fifty or more players.

As often as not, with as many as a dozen or more musicians appearing on stage with little direction, egos would take over and individual players would play two, three, even four choruses each. Hence one tune would be stretched out to last for almost half an hour, leaving ten minutes remaining for a final number. The attention spans of audiences were never as long as the performing musicians would have liked them to be.

At one of Dick Gibson's Denver Jazz Extravaganzas in the late '70s, I gained insight into the jazz audience. After a so-so set in which I strummed my guitar, the schedule listed twenty minutes by me. Alone. *Gulp.* How could I win over several hundred glassy-eyed, half-asleep, middle-aged tipplers? I probably couldn't, but "the show must go on."

Whereupon I adjusted a vocal mic, strummed a few chords, and launched into a swingy rendition of "The Lady's in Love with You." That seemed to wake the audience. I followed it with a comic monologue on why the well-bred, educated Englishman could not sing the blues convincingly, winding up with Fats

Waller's "I'm Crazy 'Bout My Baby." The applause, as they say, was deafening. Grown men and women began to chant my name: "Marty, Marty, Marty," as if I was a candidate running for office on a "Repeal the Income Tax" ticket. Graciously bowing to the will of my fans, I gave them an encore, but I cannot recall what it was. Soon enough my twenty minutes of fame receded from the minds of my auditors, and the next cattle call of musicians mounted the bandstand.

I hardly considered myself a vocalist. I had learned to sing to survive, and not having a great voice, I stuck mostly to material that I could deliver in a tongue-in-cheek manner. In this I followed the lighthearted, humorous style of one of my idols, Fats Waller, who in addition to being a superb pianist and composer of dozens of hit songs, was also a masterful interpreter of lightweight pop songs, which he often transformed into classic standards.[2]

---

2   E.g.: "I'm Gonna Sit Right Down and Write Myself a Letter," "It's a Sin to Tell a Lie," "Your Feets Too Big," "Two Sleepy People." Fats' own "The Joint is Jumpin,'" "Ain't Misbehavin,'" "Honeysuckle Rose," "Squeeze Me," "Keepin' Out of Mischief Now," and "Black and Blue" all became classics.

CHAPTER 21

Nice Jazz Festival

In the late 1970s and early '80s, I traveled to the Nice Jazz Festival in France, where I not only performed with Soprano Summit, but also in various combinations. The festival posted scores of well-known players. The venues were outdoor stages. The sets were about forty-five minutes to an hour long. One set featured three guitars: the famous George Barnes; Vinnie Corrao, a New Jersey bebop player; and me. George and Vinnie were plugged in. Indeed George Barnes, along with his rival Les Paul, was one of the earliest proponents of the amplified guitar.

As our set progressed, I began to notice that whenever I took a solo, the audience applauded. When George or Vinnie played: silence. Strange. Why was I getting hands and they weren't? I was beginning to feel uncomfortable. The famous George Barnes shunned? How could this happen? It turned out that the Nice soundmen were unable to hook up the wires from the American instruments. I, on the other hand, was picked up by an ordinary European microphone on a boom that fed into the loudspeaker system.

It should be said that the French audiences seemed to believe that only black musicians were able to play jazz. White players were considered second-rate imitators who neither understood nor grasped the essence of the music.

The early years of the twentieth century witnessed the inception of a philosophy which the French dubbed *négritude*. They, as well as a majority of Americans, were convinced that blacks were born with traits that made them superior to other races in swinging, that is expressing a superior sense of time, and an ability to express their emotions in an unfettered manner not available to other races, especially not Caucasians. According to the French, even those white musicians who had adopted the language of black jazz improvisation could never master the black sense of rhythm and melodic abandon. With one important exception: If you were *French*, you understood the essence of black music, whatever that was.

This theory was, of course, a lot of claptrap, not borne out by my experience.[1] In Nice, cornetist Bobby Hackett, idolized by musicians of all colors and persuasions, was largely ignored by the French audiences. Back in the United States, Miles Davis, the "Dark Prince" of jazz/pop, would hide in a dark corner, incognito, to hear Hackett. Dizzy Gillespie, the seminal bop trumpeter, would show up at Bobby Hackett's venue at the Henry Hudson Hotel and sit in on piano.

---

1   In Chicago's Blackstone Hotel, our quintet had two black players and might have had three had we been able to find the right guitarist.

In the 1920s, young white jazz musicians were smitten with the playing of black artists such as Louis Armstrong; pianist Earl Hines; clarinetist Jimmy Noone; drummer Baby Dodds; the Harlem stride pianists Fats Waller, James P. Johnson, and Willie "The Lion" Smith; and many more. In turn, black musicians admired such white jazzmen as cornetist Bix Beiderbecke, saxophonist Bud Freeman, guitarist Eddie Lang, and trombonist Jack Teagarden. Black singers Bessie Smith and Ethel Waters, for example, were admired and copied by their white sisters, while white pianists imitated the styles of black players Fats Waller, Art Tatum, Teddy Wilson, and Earl Hines, all four of whom were acquainted with the classical keyboard repertoire of composers like Bach, Chopin, Beethoven, and Debussy.

CHAPTER 22

Adventures in South Africa

After the Nice Jazz Festival, Bob Wilber, Kenny Davern, and I flew to South Africa where we were scheduled to perform several concerts, beginning in Durban and moving to Johannesburg. We were supplied with a local bassist and a local drummer, both of whom were clueless. They couldn't even handle a simple twelve-bar blues. Bob, Kenny, and I gritted our teeth and muddled through, getting solace from the local rotgut called "Cane."

South Africa was "cloud cuckoo land" back then.

Before landing on our flight in from France, a voice from the cockpit had admonished us to leave any salacious magazines on the plane, since publications such as *Playboy*, *Hustler*, and *Penthouse* were barred in the country. However, the front pages of the local newspapers bore stories about the ongoing divorce trial of the white mayor of Johannesburg and his white wife, who was accused of carrying on an affair with her black chauffeur. It was alleged that she would uncover the fetching parts of her anatomy while riding in the back seat, to the delight of her driver who ogled her in his rearview mirror.

Once I tried to take a commuter bus from downtown Durban to the part where our hotel was located. First a bus bearing the legend *Swartz* (black) wouldn't let me on, then the next bus, labeled *Nie Blankies* (non-whites) came along. It only took Indians and other Asians. After being passed up by several more buses, I got a cab which was plastered with salacious photos of large-bosomed white women.

On another occasion, several local jazz musicians took us to dinner. One of them kept mentioning "The King." "How's 'The King'?" "Have you seen 'The King'?" "'The King's' the greatest." It turned out he was referring to the black Canadian pianist Oscar Peterson, who was his idol. No sooner had he finished singing Peterson's praises, then he turned around and excoriated our black waiter for bringing him the wrong drink, loudly calling him names and telling him to return to the stupid village he had come from.

We wound up staying in South Africa about two weeks, during which time we heard much more racial degradation.

As the airplane transporting us away from South Africa reached cruising speed, I felt that I had never been so happy to leave a place. When I had left Nazi Germany, I was too young to understand what an ugly place it was becoming. I had no doubts about South Africa's ugliness.

CHAPTER 23

―――――

Eisbein mit Sauerkraut

It wasn't long before I was on my way back to Europe, this time with a package celebrating the music of Louis Armstrong. Three trumpets performed orchestrated solos taken from some of Armstrong's greatest recorded performances. With Kenny Davern on clarinet and Ed Hubble on trombone, they replicated the functions of those instruments on the records.

The rhythm section consisted of Bob Rosengarden, drums; George Duvivier on bass; me on guitar and banjo; and the leader, Dick Hyman, on piano. Dick was a keyboard virtuoso who knew thousands of tunes, all of which he performed with accuracy and verve. He could write music almost faster than some of us could play it. Blanche Thomas, a "fat mama" singer from New Orleans, and Ruby Braff, a clever cornet stylist, were added attractions.

The three trumpeters who rendered the orchestrated Armstrong solos were led by Jimmy Maxwell, who had played lead trumpet for three-and-a-half years for the demanding Benny Goodman; Pee Wee Erwin, another veteran of the Goodman Orchestra and later the Tommy Dorsey Orchestra; and Joe Newman, who had graced the trumpet sections of the Lionel Hampton and Count Basie orchestras.

We played versions of some famous Armstrong classics: "Heebie-Jeebies," "Muskrat Ramble," "Willie the Weeper," "Struttin with Some Barbecue," "West End Blues," to name a few. Blanche Thomas sang "You've Been a Good Old Wagon (But You Done Broke Down)." Ruby Braff played "Hustling and Bustling for Baby" and bad-mouthed everybody in the ensemble, and in the audience, and in the world, as was his style.

When we played to a good house in Berlin, I was asked to say a few words in German, which I did. The audience liked it, and so did the newspaper critics. After the concert a fan took me to an old-style Berlin restaurant where I indulged in *eine echt Berliner Spezialität, Eisbein mit Sauerkraut und Erbsenpüree* accompanied by several shots of *Bommerlunder,* a local Schnapps.

This was boiled pork hock. *Erbsenpüree* is mashed yellow peas. Eating this type of diet can potentially clog one's arteries worse than traffic clogs the Holland Tunnel at rush hour. I haven't dined on it since.

Our tour took us to Zagreb (then in Yugoslavia; now in Croatia), Paris (lukewarm reception, "not enough black musicians"), Barcelona, Genoa, Rome, and Bologna. In Bologna I noticed pretty women strolling the main street. They were elegantly attired in the latest styles that would have turned heads in Palm Beach or on Rodeo Drive. When I remarked on their chic to a cab driver, he said, "Streetwalkers." One never knows.

Marty with trumpeter Ruby Braff, Italy, mid-1970s

CHAPTER 24

Windows on the World

In the late 1970s, I moved my family to Brooklyn, to a duplex in Carroll Gardens which, if I had held onto it, would have made me a rich man. While we lived there, I worked in a trio at the Windows on the World at the very top of the World Trade Center. Dill Jones, a transplanted Welshman, played piano and ran the group, which also included Bill Pemberton on bass and me on guitar. Another pianist played when we were on our breaks.

We followed a bizarre schedule. After experiencing the world's longest elevator ride – actually, we had to take two elevators to reach the top – we would play for 20 minutes, take 15 minutes off, play for 15 minutes, take 20 minutes off, play for 30 minutes, take 20 minutes off, play for 10 minutes, take 10 minutes off – you get the idea. It was an uneven schedule that in the half-year that I worked there, I never could get memorized, nor did Dill or Bill. On our longest break, Dill and I would dash for the elevators to get to the ground floor, where the bartender would have our drinks waiting for us (the drinks at Windows on the World were too expensive). We would gulp them down, make a run for the elevators, and get back just in the nick of time.

Late one evening, we were playing our final number when Imelda Marcos, wife of the Philippine president, showed up with Van Cliburn, the classical pianist, and an entourage of be-medalled and be-ribboned Philippine officers. The place was now closed, but of course they were seated and catered to. The entourage wanted to dance, so we provided the music even though our time was up. It was an occasion when I was glad that we had a union contract so we could get overtime pay. The hat-check girl and waiters weren't as fortunate. The Marcos party members were lousy tippers.

CHAPTER 25

Classic Jazz Quartet

At the close of the 1970s, I became one-quarter of the Classic Jazz Quartet. Dick Wellstood, a fine pianist with an enviable reputation, was our musical keystone. Dick Sudhalter, co-author of *Bix, Man and Legend*, a biography of the legendary cornetist Leon "Bix" Beiderbecke, and *Lost Chords*, a book calling attention to neglected jazz musicians, played cornet. Joe Muranyi, Louis Armstrong's last clarinet player, joined up, and I pumped out rhythm on the guitar.

When we met to rehearse, we spent as much time searching for a name as we spent working on learning our repertoire. Weeks went by devoted to debating the aptness of Hot Four, Gotham Stompers, Rhythmakers, New York Swingers, Penthouse Playboys: one cheesy appellation after another. I suggested that rock groups used any number of names that had nothing to do with their music, such as the Grateful Dead, The Rolling Stones, Led Zeppelin, etc.

After several weeks I hit upon a name that would get us noticed: The Bourgeois Scum. Whereupon large grins, knee slaps, and terms such as Great! Perfect! That's it! came from my colleagues. Now that we had a name, we could rehearse.

Dick Sudhalter, who had worked as a newspaper correspondent in Europe and wrote on jazz for New York newspapers, mentioned the name to Jonathan Schwartz. Schwartz played highbrow pop music for WNYC, New York Public Radio.

According to Dick, Schwartz became quite agitated upon hearing the quartet's proposed name, asserting that he would never mention it over the air.

"Did Schwartz give a reason?" I asked.

"No," replied a crestfallen Dick.

"He probably doesn't know what 'bourgeois' means, and there are several definitions of 'scum,' and the title probably strikes him as being political and smacking of hippie culture."

Ergo, the four of us huddled and came up with The Classic Jazz Quartet, a name about as exciting as a lukewarm sitz bath.

As it turned out, we played a few gigs, cut a couple of LPs, and gradually the four of us became involved in separate projects.

CHAPTER 26

The Orphan Newsboys

For a year I played Monday nights at an East Side saloon called Michael's Pub with a trad band that featured the squawkings of Woody Allen's clarinet. Mondays were the pub's busiest night. Customers piled in – not to hear Woody's juvenile efforts, but to see him. He often appeared late while the band was already playing, and sometimes not at all. When he showed up, they saw a little millionaire in shabby clothing who seldom, if ever, altered his saturnine expression. During intermissions Woody would sometimes join the musicians in a side room, rarely conversing, sometimes reading a novel or trying out a clarinet reed. The best one could say about his musical efforts was that he tried. Did he enjoy playing with the band? Who could tell. He never altered his gloomy visage.

And then one Monday night, as we were grinding through a hoary old barbershop quartet favorite, "Won't You Come Home

The Orphan Newsboys sometime in the 80s or early '90s.
Greg Cohen, bass; Bobby Gordon, clarinet; Peter Ecklund trumpet,
Marty Grosz, guitar. Gibson L-S with a post-1935 tail-piece.
Probably in Kobe, Japan.

Bill Bailey," John, the leader, pointed to me to take a banjo solo. Twang! On the very first beat of my chorus, a string broke, throwing the other three strings out of tune. Woody cracked up, his usual sourpuss beaming with mirth and chortling as he held his side with the hand that wasn't clutching his clarinet. The other musicians were taken aback. What was so funny? It wasn't as if I was in Carnegie Hall with a spotlight on me. The pianist took over as I fished a string out of my pocket and proceeded to affix it to my banjo's tailpiece. After our set was over, I wondered if perhaps the incident reminded Woody of a silent-movie gag, like the ones that Chaplin or Buster Keaton would have used.

In the meantime I had assembled a quartet composed of several of my favorite musicians: Peter Eklund, a trumpet player with a lovely tone and a hot sense of rhythm; Bobby Gordon, a soulful clarinetist in whose quintet I had played twenty years earlier in Chicago; Greg Cohen, a most talented bass player who was handy with a bow as well as plucking solid time. I sang ditties, strummed rhythm, and looked for bookings. I dubbed the quartet the Orphan Newsboys for no reason except that the name might get attention. Orphaned newsboys had been characters in melodramas and songs at the turn of the century.

It wasn't long before the four of us were hired to play for an Alaskan cruise. Our wives and girlfriends could come along gratis and did. This particular cruise was focused on gourmet dining.

As our liner cruised along shores covered with millions of Alaskan spruce trees, middle-aged passengers stuffed themselves with gourmet fare that rivaled that of Trimalchio's feast in ancient Rome. The menu could have been written by Marcel Proust. Two days of this hyper-gormandizing and my wife and I were ready

Marty with Milt Hinton, 1980s

Marty with bassist and composer Bob Haggart

for hardtack. As soon as our ship docked at a port, we dashed off in search of a diner, where she had a toasted-cheese sandwich and I, a tuna salad on rye.

I had played several cruises before, in the Caribbean, and found them to be silly ways to waste time and money. Trips with no purpose except self-indulgence, they quickly become boring and useless. Unless, of course, you are earning a living by catering to passengers' wishes. Given a choice, I'd rather play for jolly dancers in a Chicago saloon (of my youth) than on a pearl-encrusted cruise liner with three swimming pools and a 24-hour bar.

I would, however, recommend Alaskan cruises for insomniacs. The combination of the ship's rocking motion and the crisp sea air puts you into a deep sleep before your head hits the pillow.

The next stops for the Orphan Newsboys were at various jazz parties in California, Florida, Illinois, Texas, Arkansas, Georgia, North Carolina, and Colorado. We even got as far as Kobe, Japan. My favorite venue was at an annual jazz weekend at Conneaut Lake, Pennsylvania, hosted by Joe Boughton, a devoted jazz fan.

The musicians and patrons were housed in an ancient hotel by an ancient amusement park. Some of the swing-era musicians who participated could remember performing at the park with big bands in the '30s. Joe's intense love of the music must have been the reason he could persuade many top-notch veterans of the swing era to perform. Other parties paid higher fees, but Joe got the likes of saxophonists Bud Freeman (ex-Benny Goodman and Tommy Dorsey), trumpeter Billy Butterfield (ex-Artie Shaw), bassist Bob Haggart (ex-Bob Crosby), guitarist George Van Eps (ex-Ray Noble), bassist Milt Hinton (ex-Cab Calloway), and pianist Dick Hyman (ex-Arthur Godfrey) to perform at his annual parties.

The 1980s and 1990s were traveling years for me. I would play with American and local musicians mostly in Europe, where I would be for months at a time. In Germany, my dear friend Nico, a bass player, would arrange tours of combined European and American players. The farthest I traveled was Australia.

CHAPTER 27

Akira Tsumura and his Banjo Collection

In the early 1980s, I was contacted by Yasuo Utsumi from Kobe, Japan. He was a guitar and banjo fan and player who loved jazz, and he wanted me to come over. I had never been to the Orient, and I accepted gladly. I was housed in a top-notch hotel, poked around Kobe, and demonstrated my playing style for him.

Yasuo introduced me to Akira Tsumura, whose wealthy family owned a prosperous company that sold all manner of natural products with medicinal properties such as dried seaweed, plankton, tree barks, plant roots, leaves, and grasses. I was invited to Mr. Tsumura's suburban home, a large impressive estate which dwarfed other houses in the neighborhood.

Mr. Tsumura showed me his extensive collection of banjos and guitars which he kept in temperature-controlled glass cases.

I saw a large glass bowl which must have contained four hundred different banjo keys, which were used to tighten the calfskin heads (similar to drum heads) of banjos. We looked through his collection of banjo music, instruction books, and elaborately decorated arch-top guitars. In one corner was a waist-high stack of 78 rpm shellac records comprised of every recording upon which Louis Armstrong appeared.

After being bedazzled by these treasures, we were driven to the city of Tokyo, to the Tsumura Building in the center of town. There I was shown further treasures.

My host pressed a button causing the wall in his office to open, revealing a collection of probably two hundred different pairs of blue jeans. Throughout the lower floors of the skyscraper hung paintings by a certain Frazetta, whose specialty seemed to be the depiction of a mystical Nordic race of bear-pelt clad women with golden locks down to their waists, wearing Dutch ovens to protect their enormous breasts. Riding giant steeds, the Amazonian women were spearing Nordic saber tooth tigers. It was all rather bizarre to me, quite different from the expected demure damsels depicted by the great Japanese printmaker Hokusai.

I was invited to dine in the company's executive dining room with Mr. and Mrs. Tsumura, an English friend of theirs who would act as interpreter, and my friend Yasuo. A waiter wearing a black tie and white gloves served us venison.

While I attempted to make polite conversation, the music of Django Reinhardt and the Hot Club of France accompanied home movies of the Tsumuras and their teenage daughter vacationing in Hawaii. As I gulped down a mouthful of wine, I thought to myself, *This is bizarre. What am I doing here? When can I get out of here?*

The following evening, I was to appear with Mr. Tsumura's band at a basement club. It was what is called a "vanity" job. There were seven musicians and a vocalist. Tsumura-san's factotum set up two banjos and a giant, gaudily inlaid guitar. It had once belonged to a famous cowboy singer, but I can't remember which one. The piano player resembled the fiendish organist in Sergei Eisenstein's film *Alexander Nevsky*. He was a grizzled old man who surveyed his surroundings with a contorted visage and piercing, watery eyes. It was difficult to ascertain what relation the dissonant, acrid ramblings that his talon-like fingers executed on the keyboard had to the language of music.

There weren't many customers. I got the feeling that the few who were there were employees of his company.

After a while, Tsumura-san appeared wearing a leather jacket with an eagle bearing the American escutcheon embossed on its back. Tsumura picked up his jumbo guitar; the band launched into a number during which he broke a string, put his guitar down, and took a seat at a table.

When a girl vocalist got up to sing, the pianist's multi-tonal, out-of-meter introduction confused her. She couldn't discern a keynote from the pianist's scramblings. The group played a few more tunes. The musicians got tumblers of Scotch. The singer asked if I would be so kind as to play an introduction for her on the next set. No problem.

I asked the amateur musicians to lay out for four measures while I brought the singer in with a proper introduction. No use. When the time came, the sputtering, teeth-gnashing pianist destroyed my modest intro by hammering the keyboard like a demented chimpanzee. I shrugged my shoulders and glanced at the singer as if to say it was hopeless. The poor girl was stymied. Whereupon the evening stumbled along with several gentlemen indulging themselves in whiskey, laughing, knocking bottles over, falling off their chairs. This sort of silly behavior, I was later told, was accepted because Japanese businessmen were so stressed that periodic benders were considered a healthy way to relieve tension.

At the end of the evening, Tsumura-san handed me an envelope containing cash. I thanked him and slipped the envelope into my jacket pocket. I did not count the contents, surmising that a man of his wealth would be trustworthy and might feel insulted if I showed doubt.

The next day I was up at 6 a.m. and wasted no time getting to Narita Airport. It wasn't until I was in the departure lounge that I counted the bills in the envelope: $10,000 US currency. $10,000 for a one-night performance? No, that couldn't be correct. However, I had heard stories about the largesse of wealthy Japanese jazz fans. The clarinetist Buddy DeFranco once told me of a fan who presented him with a *Patek Philippe* watch. My wife and I could certainly use some cash to make repairs on our crumbling home in Piermont, New York.

It took exactly two days before I received a phone call from a certain Mr. Hiroshige who informed me that I had been given Mr. Tsumura's American cash envelope by mistake. I was supposed to receive two or three hundred dollars; I don't recall the exact amount. But okay, I made a little more than that at other Japanese venues, and I had opened up a market. I took out my fee and returned the balance to an address in California.

CHAPTER 28

My Guitars

I play two acoustic arch-top guitars. They were made at the Gibson Guitar Company plant in Kalamazoo, Michigan, in 1927 and 1928. At the start of the twentieth century, guitars had flat tops and oval sound holes and were strung with either gut or metal strings. They came in models for flamenco and classical music and were usually strung with gut strings for use in mandolin orchestras and for solo performances. At the close of the nineteenth century, the banjo came into favor in small ensembles because it was louder than the guitar. To give the guitar more volume and presence, the Gibson company developed a guitar whose shape was modeled after that of a cello. The arch top produced more volume and a tone that blended with the other rhythm instruments: bass or tuba, piano, and drums.

Arch-top guitars were used in dance bands and favored

Marty with Buckey Pizzarelli

by jazz musicians. They were strummed with picks of tortoise shell or celluloid.

With the introduction of electrical amplification, the traditional guitar shape, which acted as a tone chamber, was no longer needed. Hence, what we see ninety percent of non-classical players using today are wooden planks with pickups. Comes a power outage and there is no sound.

I favor clear, direct, unaltered sound. Mechanical distortions of tone and pitch are dishonest. I was initially drawn to the guitar because the other musicians in a jazz group had to lay out, or reduce their volume, to enable the guitar to be heard. I delighted in the moment of softness, the contrast that I heard.

I have strummed my guitars all over the United States, Europe, Japan, Australia, in Africa, even in the White House. My discography, compiled by a jazz scholar, is 100 pages long.

The most pleasure I've gotten out of playing was in a series of jobs where I played for dancing. In the late 1970s and early 1980s, Dick Wellstood, a fine pianist, hired me to play in a sextet that furnished music for dancing at various country club and yacht clubs in New Jersey. We had six musicians: trumpet, tenor sax (doubling clarinet), piano, acoustic string bass, acoustic guitar, and drums. We played foxtrots slow and fast, and an occasional rhumba or a waltz.

There were no announcements, no features, no vocals. We musicians could concentrate on music and rhythm; no cheesy showbiz, no "Now we'd like to feature our (fill in the instrumentalist)." Just melody, harmony, and rhythm.

Heaven.

PART II

The Interviews

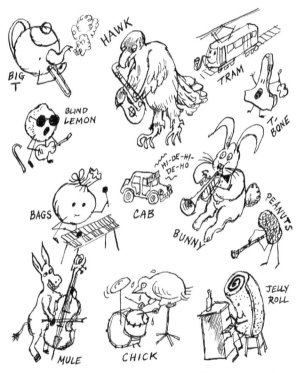

BIG T- JACK TEAGARDEN ; BLIND LEMON JEFFERSON ; HAWK- COLEMAN HAWKINS;
TRAM - FRANK TRUMBAUER ; T- BONE : T-BONE WALKER ; BAGS - MILT JACKSON ;
CAB - CAB CALLOWAY ; BUNNY- BUNNY BERIGAN ; MULE -MAJOR HOLLEY ;
CHICK- CHICK WEBB ; JELLY ROLL - JELLY-ROLL MORTON , PEANUTS - MIKE HUCKO

My cartoons on the nicknames of jazz players.

Illustration and captions by Marty Grosz

Marty Grosz has an extraordinary gift for connecting with audiences. Given a mic, he can instantly deliver fantastical, meandering musings on music, history, love, and the human condition. Sometimes, to the delight of his listeners, he gets so lost in his stories that he forgets which tune he intended to introduce.

The following "greatest hits" compilations, gathered from interviews with Marty between 2015 and 2019, hint at what it's like to hear him live. Don't let the subject headings fool you: true to form, each story contains layers within layers.

On Guitar Tuning

Plowman: Did you own guitars back then [in the mid-1940s]?

Grosz: I had a four-string guitar at the time. I had given up the six-string guitar because it wasn't going anywhere for me. I loved stride piano, I loved "The Lion," Fats, James P., Joe Sullivan, the rest.

I also wanted more bass. And four-string banjos stop at C below middle C. That's as low as it gets. And that's not low enough for me. So there was a guy in New York, I'd had his records since I was a teenager. Carl Kress. He made a solo album, the first jazz guitar player to do anything like that. Three 78 sides were put in an album by Decca, and these were original compositions by Kress. It was really a kind of unusual thing for a jazz guy to do this.

He was extremely busy in the studios and he used a tuning of fifths, from the bottom up, B♭ F C G D A, with the A dropped an octave. He could also play regular Spanish tuning. And he was very gifted. So I got the idea, since I'd been playing banjo and actually even studied it a bit. I didn't have a teacher but I got tips from guys. I also got some books and tried to work out some solos and licks. So I thought, *Hmm, I'll get a six-string guitar, and I'll tune it something like Kress, except it'll be too confusing. So I'll keep my top four strings like a plectrum banjo, and I'll add two bass strings in fifths.* That's how it's been ever since.

Plowman: So you totally circumvented Spanish tuning?

Grosz: Yes. That's how I got into this whole thing.

On Finding the Right Notes

Grosz: Good guys like Pee Wee Russell find it instantly, the note that the other guys aren't playing. It's barbershop quartet harmony, is really is what it is.

Plowman: I find a lot of the time with [young] guys my age, when they try to do it, it's like two squiggly lines hit each other and don't really dance around each other, as opposed to being—

Grosz: Well the first thing you do is take a tune like "Mood Indigo" and you find your harmony notes [*sings trombone melody*]. You know, if it's on the third, somebody's gotta take the fifth, then somebody takes the root, and start that way. Then later on you can decide, you can get fancy. And you got three horns, there's only so many possibilities. Should you leave out the root and just use, like the melody's on the major seventh, use the fifth, and something else, a ninth or something. You know, you try different combinations that'll work. Ellington used very simple harmonies on that, but he got that effect because he had the trumpet with a mute. It all depended on the mutes, playing [*sings trumpet melody*].

Plowman: And that was the highest voice, right?

Grosz: That was the highest voice. And then he had high trombone [*sings*] underneath him with a mute, and then an octave and a half down or so was the clarinet. It all had to do with, you could only do it with a microphone, over a microphone. You see pictures of those guys in 1932 playing this thing, they're always standing up by a microphone. Cause clarinet will die, you won't hear it. I mean in a big broadcast or in a room.

Plowman: It's all about pitching for the instrument.

Grosz: Yeah, and that damn thing [“Mood Indigo”] was on the jukebox for twenty years, so help me. That tune, so slow, the original version, three horns and four rhythm. I mean if you can consider a banjo player a rhythm. I never heard real musical notes out of him, I don't know what he—

Plowman: Which guy?

Grosz: Freddie Guy, Ellington's banjo player. *Blak blak blak* [*banjo noise*] All you hear is *blak blak blak*. You never hear any tone.

Plowman: I like him. It's part of the sound.

Grosz: Yeah, but what did he use for a head, a paper bag? Wrapping paper? You at least expect to hear a little bit of *bloongg*. It's a banjo, it's not gonna ring like a guitar, you know that. But his is really sort of *blak blak, blak blak, blak*. [*knocks on table*] Hello! Yeah. He wasn't a great swinger, he was a rather weak...and that was Ellington's big trouble, the rhythm section. It sort of *blak blak blak*'ed along. It didn't really dig in, in a sense.

But they had a lot of tone color, they had a lot of colors. Sonny Greer, much to my surprise, obviously had it in him, but just didn't do it, I don't know. He made one record with Lionel Hampton, "Ring Dem Bells," and he takes a break – wonderful – and he's playing [*sings drum break*] – and Sonny Greer is wailing, you know, it sounds great. But he's with John Kirby on bass, he's got a couple of very strong rhythm players.

Plowman: Yeah, Sonny does not get enough credit.

Grosz: Well, he was with Ellington for the longest time. What's very interesting to me was to hear broadcasts that somebody took off the radio of the Ellington band. I had one, I still probably have it someplace, I don't know where. But it's 1942, and they're in Colorado Springs. What did the band do? The Ellington band clearly did not play "The Flaming Sword" and [*sings*] "Cottontail." Yeah, well they didn't play those on dance gigs. That was a special showbiz performance at a club with dancers and all that stuff.

Anyway, it's broadcasting [*radio broadcast voice*] "*Ladies and gentlemen, at the Timbers (or something) in Colorado Springs*" – it's 1942, war's just been declared, you know – and they're playing "Tangerine" right from a stock. "*Quick write me a "Tangerine" – Hey boss.*" You know. He had guys who wrote for him, quick slap it together. It sounds to me like they're playing it from a stock. But there again, the first chorus of "Tangerine," he's got Tricky Sam Nanton playing it.

Now, "Tangerine" was a big hit for Jimmy Dorsey. Boy and girl. Boy sings "*Tangerine, she is all they claim, with her eyes of night, and lips as bright as flaaame.*" And Dorsey had this gimmick that worked, made a lot of money for him at that time [*sings shout chorus and saxophone solo*] – that's all he had to do on it, just to show that he was Jimmy Dorsey. He usually had four bars or six bars of *doodly doodly doodly*. He'd do some tricky stuff, then it was "*Tangerine, she is (girl vocalist, Helen O'Connell) she is all they claim*." The kids loved it, you know. Big hit. But he [Ellington] has *yah yah yah* – Tricky Sam [*laughs*], it's really great, it's so out there, you know.

Plowman: Sure, I bet nobody really cared.

Grosz: They were dancing. It was war time. Who cares about anything? You care about [*pounds fist to hand*]. That's what you really care about.

****

Grosz: So I got this cheesy wartime Harmony guitar, *ugh*. Had no sound at all, but I didn't know that. And I remember I got a little disappointed. I didn't know anything. I didn't know where you put your fingers, nothing. And I started to see those little boxes they had on sheet music. And of course they were all wrong.

Plowman: The fret markers?

Grosz: Well they had the dots where you put your fingers. A D7th chord, every chord was with six notes usually, and that isn't what people use, and it was difficult. I sweated through that until I got to talking with some guys, or I saw some guys.

You know it was hard, 'cause the only place you'd ever see a guitar player was with a big band. So I'd go to all the movie houses and see the big bands. All the ones that

I could get out of school or somehow manage to see. I saw some good ones. I saw Basie.

But you know you're sitting back from the orchestra, there's a guy in a band jacket with a guitar in his lap, you're not gonna see much of what's going on. When I got to be like 15, 16, I looked old enough that, with the older guys, I could get into clubs. You know the drinking age was 18 in New York. So then you could get into some of the clubs, especially since the clubs were all the ones in the Village. All of them of course were run by hoods. By the Mafiosos. You could go in and you could see some of these guys, and you could actually hear them a little bit.

So one of the guys that I could see and hear a little bit was Eddie Condon, who had a four-string guitar tuned like a plectrum banjo, 27-inch scale. Tenor banjo has a 23-inch scale. It's tuned like a viola and the neck isn't much longer than a viola neck. The plectrum banjo was the original American banjo. I don't know where it got its tuning, the five-string banjo. I never understood what the fifth string really did, but they all had 'em. So him [Eddie] you could hear, sometimes, and you could certainly see him. And you could get an idea.

Eddie Condon

Plowman: You told me that your dad knew Eddie Condon. Can I hear that story?

Grosz: My old man certainly liked jazz, what he thought jazz was. And later on, he'd play some of my records, and you know, get his vino and a cigarillo and *ahhh* [*mimes back of head on hand while leaning back*], you know, and enjoy them.

There's an anecdote, it's not much of an anecdote, but he told me how he and Erich Maria Remarque – the guy who wrote *All Quiet on the Western Front* – they were old buddies from Germany – my old man wanted to hear some jazz. And they wound up at Eddie Condon's down on 47 West 3rd St. The whole area doesn't exist anymore. It's all NYU now, new buildings and stuff. Anyway, I said, "Oh yeah, how'd you like it, Pop?" [*thick German accent*] "Yeah! I liked ze cubist guitar!" It was clever, he thought. Over the door, hanging like a shield, but not a shield, with neon lights was a cubistic little guitar with about three strings on it. You know, the idea of the guitar. He's telling me this, I'm home for a few days, I'm at the house and I'm eating breakfast, and my mother's there and apparently she had heard the story. And he's telling it, about how he wanted them to play the "Georgia Cakewalk." [*hums march*]

Plowman: Your dad wanted Eddie Condon to play it?

Grosz: Yeah! I mean it's almost a march in sections [*scats all the separate sections*]. So he asked the waiter, "Could you ask the band to play the 'Georgia Cakewalk?'" And it was Wild Bill Davison, I don't know who the clarinet player was, probably Cutty Cutshall on trombone, Condon, I guess it was Jack Lesberg in those days on bass. Anyway, that tune, you encountered it once in a while. So the waiter said, "You know sir, I think you oughta buy the band a drink." And so the old man, feeling no pain, bought the band a drink.

My mother's already in her head thinking, "How many guys in the band? Seven, eight?" *Cha-ching*, you know? [*chuckles*] And Condon didn't play it! And Pop sent them another drink. "Tell them I'm the guy who asked for the 'Georgia Cakewalk.'" And they did play it, finally. Dad said, "Boy oh boy, zey really give it ze business, I'm telling you!" To him it was worth it. To my mother it was [*looks alarmed at pocket book*].

Plowman: Did your dad make friends with Eddie Condon?

Grosz: Friends? Condon, you see, his father was a saloon keeper in Momence, Indiana. Right off the boat, I guess. Irishman. And he didn't do this [*imitates bartender pouring drinks*]. He had people doing that for him. His old man ran the joint and would sit with the customers. [*Irish accent*] "How are ya, Garry? Haven't seen ya in a while!" You know, "How's the missus" and all that shit. "Oh, well, [*nods sympathetically*] there'll be hard times," you know, like a host.

And that's where Condon got it from. And he was very successful at it. He had a million and one jokes, lines. Despite the fact that guys put him down because [*Brooklyn accent*] "Ah, he's the guy plays the four-string guitar." Jeez, what the fuck. He had small hands! He could not have done justice to a real six string guitar, I don't think.

And I will say, you have to give Condon credit. I know nowadays this is all discredited, it's all considered crap, jazz began with Charlie Parker, and so forth and so on. And the establishment, they don't make their money by getting you to listen to old stuff, they get their money by encouraging everybody to join in stage bands with five saxes and four trombones and all that stuff, playing Sal Nistico charts or somebody else, I don't know who it is now. Doing that kind of stuff. And then they can lament why nobody likes jazz.

But Condon was good. He was put down by a lot of guys, "Aah, he's playing four-string guitar, aah." He absolutely knew every song that was ever written, it seems. Really, I mean it's just not me. I've talked to other guys who worked with him.

And he never played a bad chord. I mean he must have had to, he must have been drunk and hit something wrong. But he had a fantastic ear for harmony. I heard him many times. And not only that, I had some fine musician friends who actually played with him, sat next to him at the club, and they said – a trombone player friend of mine who played fine trombone, also played piano, said, "I never heard him make a mistake, I never heard him play a bad chord." And Bob Wilber, who also was schooled, played soprano and tenor and clarinet and everything, fine musician, said the same thing. "I played there for, you know, a year, I never heard Condon play a wrong chord."

And he played every kind of damn tune you want. He had a fast ear and a lightning memory. I mean how many people, even fifty or forty years ago, knew a song called "Have You Ever Seen a Dream Walking"? Well they had medleys, and they'd play a couple of sets with an opener, or they'd play another tune, then they'd have a medley where the clarinet player would pick a tune, then the trumpet and the trombone, and maybe the bass player'd do a thing – and I'd come to hear the strangest tunes for, I hate the term, a Dixieland band, but nothing stopped it. Nothing stopped Condon. "I've Got a Right to Sing the Blues," that's got a lot of changes in it if you do it right.

And one time I came in, they're doing "September Song," "The Way You Look Tonight." I mean nothing stopped them, and he knew them all. They didn't have arrangements, everything was ear. But he picked up on them. When he played with the Summa Cum Laude band, which did have arrangements, some of them [the players] had arrangements or charts, but he didn't have any. And when he played with Bobby Hackett's big band, he didn't have a book. He just played by ear. He didn't take solos, particularly, he wasn't interested.

Plowman: How much did you get to see him play?

Grosz: Eh, off and on, you know, I'd talk to him. He knew that I liked, that I was a fan, and he sort of indulged me. When I got older, I started cracking wise, and you know, he was the wisecracker. And he'd known everyone. God, he'd made records with Louis Armstrong very early, in 1929. That wasn't early for Louie, but it was early for white guys, you know, playing with Louie. And as soon as he got to New York which was in '28, he recorded with Fats Waller. And Fats said of him, "He plays more on four strings than some guys play on six." He had a terrific memory and he had a terrific ear, and between the two of them you couldn't beat him. Of course, you know, guitar players, a lot of them would put him down because it was four strings as opposed to six. And I understand that.

Plowman: Is Condon the "guy" for four-string guitar?

Grosz: Well, whatever he did worked, and a lot of musicians liked it. And subsequently a lot of people put him down because he was a "moldy fig," or it was what they call, a term I hate, Dixieland. Because you know, time marches on and the new gang always thinks the old gang was terrible. That's the way progress works. You put Grandpa and Grandma out in the woodshed or out in the county home. And the new bunch moves in. And that's the way the world works.

INTERVIEW 4

Drummers and Bassists

Plowman: Who are some of your favorite drummers you've played with?

Grosz: I told you, Vernel Fournier! I played with him once. Once. And you somehow know this. It isn't cerebral, it's not in the cortex. It's someplace. You sit down and you play with the guy, and no matter what the hell it is you're playing, it's right. It feels right. The time is right. I've played with guys who are way too much on top. *Push push push.* And then you play with guys who are way too much laid back. You've had the experience, you know.

Vernel Fournier felt just right.

There was a guy in Chicago named Bob Cousins who got a day job. His beat was right. It was the beat. That's the way they used to talk about it.

So with Vernel, it was just a gig, something that [Dick] Sudhalter put together – which meant the trumpet was made out of cream cheese. I liked Dick, but he wasn't really…and he thought he was Bix, like a lot of other guys. And I saw this ragged-ass guy, looked like he slept under the bridge, had some kind of jacket on, was all [*gives ruffled*

Marty with bassist Major Holley
and cornetist Tom Saunders, Stuttgart, 1980s

motion] and I thought, *No, it can't be*. And I'd seen him in Chicago with the Ahmad Jamal trio, and I said, "*It can't be*." But it was. And he started playing and it just – I said, *That's it*. It was right.

I always used to like – of course I never played with him – that Billy Taylor, the one that played with Ellington. He's on the first Fats Waller records, "Sweetie Pie" and stuff. [*imitates swinging bass line in two*] You know, they show how you can make "two" swing. Usually two is a jazz musician's nightmare.

Oh, there are guys – Milt Hinton for example – wasn't really right. He was too much on top. Too eager. Too aggressive. Which is fine. You know, you don't wanna panty-waist back there. Different people get different sounds.

Major Holley and I got along. I liked him. He was pretty good with the bow and everything. I liked Major. And we had fun together. He was relaxed. People used to criticize Milt 'cause Milt always wanted to play on top, an eager beaver, you know? Even as an old man, he's *ding ding ding ding ding ding* [*imitates frantic quarter notes on bass*]. Once in a while you just gotta go *doom be doom be doom be doom* [*imitates relaxed "two" feel on bass*]. It's very comforting, you know?

I must say I also liked Major because, we're down in Florida, and there's all these guys – Terry Gibbs, all these *names* – and for some reason they made Major the leader of a set. So Major says, "I'm gonna play so and so, and he points to me, 'Marty, play an intro.'" Some kind of swing tune. I don't know what it was. And I go something like *booka chinka chinka plink* and all of a sudden I got [*imitates drums piano bass all coming in behind him*]. And Major all of a sudden says "HOLD IT, HOLD IT." And all these guys are looking at him, and he says "I said GUITAR intro, okay? Let's do it again." And I felt embarrassed, in a sense, because I didn't have anything that great to lay down, you know? I wasn't Django Reinhardt, come on! [*laughs*] But still, I gave him credit for it. He had a certain thing in his head. And sometimes that's nice, when you have a little guitar mouse, and the whole rest of the musical menagerie comes roaring in. It can be a nice effect. Instead of just endless piano intros – it's always a piano intro. The thing with the bass player and the drummer joining in – even though they didn't know what the fuck he was gonna play.

Plowman: It's still like that, times have not changed.

Grosz: Jeezus.

INTERVIEW 5

Slam Stewart

Plowman: While we're talking about bassists, can you tell about my favorite, Slam [Stewart]?

Grosz: I played with him a handful of times, and it was not under the best circumstances. It was a bunch of disparate people. [*forlornly*] "You want a piano introduction on this one?" "Ok…" You know, that kind of thing.

But I remember something that stuck with me always. It was Slam playing "Just One of Those Things" with the latter-day Benny Goodman sextet, Mike Bryan on guitar, Morey Feld on drums, Red Norvo on vibes, the "Slipped Disc" band, you know? And, it might have been what's his name on piano, the guy that wrote "Mission to Moscow" – Mel Powell. I remember I couldn't see the piano player.

Plowman: You saw them live?

Grosz: Yes, on stage. And what really got to me was Slam's rhythm playing. His time. And then later on I always heard it in my head. I thought, [*incredulously*] *I gotta have it wrong.* And they played it lightly. Morey Feld was a wonderful brush player. They danced. [*imitates light, dancing drum and bass playing*] You know, it wasn't *dong dong dong dong dong*, which every other bass player was doing. Slam was playing it mostly in "two." And forty years go by, and I

"We found the novelty shop in Columbus, Ohio.
Late at night we'd get slap-happy and amuse (I think) ourselves."

think, *This can't have been.* All the guys were playing in "four" those days, you know? It was the hip thing. And then I heard the [Goodman] record. I was so impressed by Slam with the "two" that it got to me somehow. Why didn't Benny get to me? Why didn't Norvo get to me? Somehow that impressed me.

Plowman: It's because you're a rhythm section guy!

Grosz: Yeah! Well, that's what I like to do best. But you can't sell that anymore. [*laughs*] So, it was about a year or two ago that I heard that record again, I said, [*sighs*] "Ahh, I was right, it was Slam and he does sound great!" It's just the right balance.

INTERVIEW 6

Mingus and the Soup

Plowman: Could you tell me your story about Mingus and the soup?

Grosz: Ah, okay. We're traveling all over Europe in a bus. The New York Jazz Repertory Company. It was under the direction of Dick Hyman, who had never been on the road. Dick Hyman was a wizard pianist, and a wizard, period, in music. The minute he got out of high school, he was in the studios, and it wasn't long before he was leading bands on the radio. Studious, serious guy, who did like jazz. His particular hobby horse was Bix [Beiderbecke]. He could talk about Bix for hours. "You know that second take on so and so…? Do you think Bix… [*mumbles*]?" And he was really a Bix specialist, which I thought was rather strange, but there you go. Anyway, Hyman had chops. So he was running these bands and transcribing arrangements off of records for, at that time, George Wein – who I never particularly liked, God bless him though.

Plowman: He got you workin'.

Grosz: Yeah! Anyway, on the road with this Louis Armstrong thing – they had been to Russia with it. And it was Yosef Neumann – Joe Newman – I used to call him that [chuckles], and Pee Wee Erwin. Maybe not known to you? Pee Wee Erwin, white trumpet player who had played with everybody. He had played with Tommy Dorsey, Benny Goodman, before that he had played with Isham Jones, Ray Noble, he had credentials. He could read, he could execute. I heard him say a couple of times, "I don't know, I did everything I could. Everything. I got drunk, I got in trouble with women, and I still couldn't sound like Bunny!"

Plowman: Bunny Berigan?

Grosz: Well Bunny Berigan, in those years, was second only to Louis Armstrong, if that, as a talent. I mean he was phenomenal. All the time smoking, drinking, never thinking of tomorrow. I mean, he didn't take care of himself. And he had Lee Wiley jumping on him every time he came to town. She was nuts about Bunny. Vocalist, Lee Wiley. Sexy little broad.

Anyway. Pee Wee said he tried all that stuff, I still couldn't sound like Bunny. And I, you know, always liked Bunny. But I never saw it this way until I read a bunch of things that Louis Armstrong said. And over the years, on four different occasions, when Louis was asked, one time quite formally by *Metronome* in 1938 or something, to list "Louis Armstrong names his favorite trumpet players," he listed Red Allen, Buck Clayton, you name 'em. Of course King Oliver. And he said, "Number one is my boy Bunny." And Berigan said the same about Louis. And Louis said in print three times, so it wasn't just, you know, an agent saying, "Hey listen. Boy are we havin' some trouble. Bunny needs all the help he can get Louie, give him a break." It wasn't that at all. He really liked Bunny.

So anyway, Pee Wee Erwin was on the tour, and he was one of the three trumpet players, Joe Newman, Pee Wee Erwin, and Jimmy Maxwell playing. I don't know if it was Hyman who did it or not, arrangements of Louie Armstrong pieces. And every time Louie Armstrong took a chorus there were three trumpets harmonized, playing the thing. Oh well. It's like Supersax. You know. It's a gimmick. I don't care, I had to be Johnny St. Cyr for "Willie the Weeper," so you know it wasn't too strenuous.

Ruby Braff was along as a, uh, trouble maker. You gotta have some pain in the ass on the tour. Oh Jeezus. Always trouble with Ruby.

Plowman: What did he get into?

Grosz: His ego! "I'm not gonna do that." "I'm not gonna play with these guys, I got my own thing." You know, just a pain in the ass. And then he'd get drunk and try to stick his tongue into your ear and stuff. Oh God.

So anyway, there we are, George Duvivier, oh yeah, Eddie Hubble – I don't know if he's still alive – playing trombone. He'd been around on the scene, he'd played with the World's Greatest Jazz Band, and he had been in an auto accident, upstate New York. And they didn't find him until the next morning, and some animal had come and chewed his foot off, so he had a fake leg, you know? Trombone player. Nice guy, played good.

Plowman: Chewed his foot off while he was alive?

Grosz: Yeah. What are you gonna do? Anyway. I used to say, "Hey come on over to the room" – we used to drink together and stuff.

And then there was Jimmy Maxwell. And Rosengarden on drums [*groans*]. Bob Rosengarden, who was a "Broadway Bob" kind of type. He knew everything about everything. "Don't do this." "Don't do that." Even Hyman was getting tired of him. I remember we were doing "Flee as a Bird to the Mountain" – you know we did early Louie. [*sings dirge*] Funeral thing, you know. I remember Duvivier coming off the stand once and saying, "Jeezus, what's he doing? It's like a burlesque show for chrissake." Oh, George didn't say for chrissake. George was a well-spoken gentleman.

So, anyway, we had a bus. It was one of those buses with the driver on the left-hand side. And up next to him was this raised seat, over part of the engine or something. And that's where Rosengarden picked for his seat. Big shot seat. Catbird seat, you know. And if you smoked [*swoons dramatically*] Rosengarden would have conniptions. And I smoked these little cigarillos once in a while. "Oh! Cigars! My father smoked cigars and stank up the whole house *blah blah blah*."

And Rosengarden was Broadway Benny. He knew everybody supposedly. He had been on the Ernie Kovacs show. And he thought of himself as Mr. Studio, and he thought he was gonna take over some band and run things. And of course what happened was, very soon that was over. The whole studio scene with all the musicians and live music. The last thing was Doc Severinsen. And that ended. What came after him, I don't know, but it got less and less important.

Plowman: So you're on tour in the bus.

Grosz: So Rosengarden was sitting there, "Oh, driver..." "Signor, what, you are talking to me?" – I'm trying to do my Italian, it's not very good. And Rosengarden's always, "Can we get going…If you see a place can we stop…" so forth and so on. And he's the big shot.

Then one day we go into the bus in the morning, and who's sitting there – he looked like Orson Welles in his latter days – Orson Welles was always wearing these capes and big coats. It was Mingus! And all of a sudden Mingus is sitting in Rosengarden's seat. And Mingus is smoking a cigar the size of a small torpedo. And there's a blue haze throughout the entire bus, and Rosengarden didn't say dick shit! I loved it. I was chortling the whole trip, you know?

And then I told you the story about the guy, one of his sidemen. I was waiting for someone in the lobby of this little hotel we were staying in in Italy. And his sideman is standing at the door to the dining room. Listening, you know… "Is he still in there?" I said, "Oh, what, what's happening?" He says, "I gotta find out if Mingus is still in there. He's still slurping his soup!" You know [*slurping noise*].

Plowman: Could you hear it?

Grosz: Yeah, you could if you were at the door. Maybe not down at the lobby. Yeah…he was strange. He played with Kid Ory and his band in Hollywood, you know, early on. And his contemporaries made fun of him. "What are you playing with those Old Tom's for?" and stuff like that. He said, "Oh man, it's a gig! They're playing music, it's all music, you know?" I kind of liked that. Although, I could see, in this business there are people you can work with more comfortably than others.

INTERVIEW 7

Bunk Johnson

Plowman: Tell me about when you heard Bunk Johnson.

Grosz: When I was fooling around during the war, I was a teenager, you know 1943, '44, Bunk Johnson and the New Orleans revival was on, and Bunk had come to New York. And that was big, big fuckin' press. They had him in *Vogue* magazine and the press. 64-year-old trumpet player. 64 years old and playing that music? Wow! You know, they thought that was fantastic. He had big press.

And Bunk did not pick the musicians he was with. The collective gang that put this band together, they picked it. And they had some of the *worst* musicians you could play with. Awful. I mean, so out of tune it'd make you cry. Almost a half-step out of tune, the trombone player. And the banjo player had to have his banjo tuned by the piano player.

The only guy that was a full-fledged, real honest player was the drummer Baby Dodds. Now Baby Dodds had been a huge influence. If you asked Gene Krupa, Dave Tough, all those guys from Chicago, the first guy they'd talk about was Baby Dodds. They said, "When we were kids we all went to wherever Baby Dodds was going to hear him play the drums." I heard a program that Mel Lewis – did you ever hear his show on WFMT? – where he talks about drummers. He talks about Dodds, where he hits the cymbal and so forth.

George Duvivier and Connie Kay

Plowman: Can you tell me a little about touring around with George Duvivier? I remember two tales you've told: one about his blood pressure, and another about when his bass was "exploded."

Grosz: Well, George Duvivier told me he was on a flight to Europe, and he wound up, by chance, sitting in a seat next to the technician who had previously taken his blood sample. He thought that was an amazing coincidence.

He [George] was visiting his mother. She lived up where Pennsylvania, New York, and New Jersey all meet. North of Manhattan, New York, up a ways. He said, "I was gonna take a nap, and I told my mother 'wake me up for the six o'clock news,'" or something. Taking a little nap in the afternoon. And he says, "The next time I woke up, I was in a hospital, looking up at that lamp in my face. And I had had the second highest blood pressure of anybody that they had a record of, that lived. I had never had blood pressure problems before, and I never had any afterwards, after I left there. After days in the hospital I was perfectly normal, and they couldn't figure out what happened. They still haven't figured it out."

And so he told me, "I'm sitting there going to Europe" – I don't know if it was particularly for our tour, or another occasion, I can't remember exactly. And who is he sitting next to by chance? The same technician that took his blood samples. And the guy says, excuse me, is your name by any chance Duvivier? Which it was. And he says, "I'm the technician that took your blood samples at the hospital." And so he [Duvivier] actually was a medical record!

What was the other story?

Plowman: About his bass exploding on tour. Why were you together, and what happened?

Grosz: We were on this Louis Armstrong tour, George was playing bass, and we were all over Europe.

Plowman: For the State Department?

Grosz: Oh, I don't know, it was for George Wein's New York Jazz Repertory Company. I guess it was State Department. Somebody had to be payin' the money. And we played in Germany, Italy, Spain, France, Scandinavia – Denmark, and Sweden, I think. And we got to Belgium, we're in Brussels, and George's bass had been opening up at the bottom. And so I think we had a day off at the hotel, and George asked me to go along with him. He said, "Hey, you wanna come along?" I said, "Yeah, I need some exercise." I wanted to see the city, you know, Brussels. And it was a Sunday, and we're looking for tape to tape up his bass at the bottom. It had come apart.

Plowman: Like they do.

Grosz: Yeah! And on Sunday, you can't go to the hardware store to get that kind of really heavy black tape, you know. And so we had to get the kind of tape you use to tape up splints and things, white medical tape. And we had to find a place. There had to be a pharmacy open at all times in Brussels, and in many cities, so that in the middle of the night or on a day off you could still...you know? So we had to find that place. And we walked all over and knocked on doors and windows of pharmacies. Finally, we find a place and the guy begrudgingly comes out. And we tried to make known that... It's interesting, trying to explain to a person who doesn't understand your language that you need some medical tape to tape up a string bass. [*laughs*]

Anyway, we got the stuff and then we took it up to the hotel. And he put it all on the table and the guys sat on the bass and pressed the bottom of it together. And it worked for a while, and then it started to come apart again. And it'd need more tape. And they would sit on it again. And finally he took it back to New York and used whatever they used to use. Horse glue, right?

Plowman: What was he like as a hang? What was he like as a player?

Grosz: Well, he knew everything. Not only did he know everything about playing, he knew everything about many things. He was the Boy Scout who got all the merit badges. I mean you're riding with him in a train – this is an aside – I remember, I'm nodding out, and he's sitting in the seat next to me and he taps me on the shoulder and says "Look!" [*past Marty stirs groggily*] We're on the train, the Talgo it was called, I think, between Spain and France. I think it was Italy? Can you go from Spain to Italy? And the gauges are different, and so the cars have these wheels. And they get on this thing and it changes the gauges of the wheels. And George, being the Boy Scout who got all the merit badges and was very interested in these things, pointed that out.

I mean, I remember we were in Toronto, and I see him in the hotel at breakfast and he says "Hey, you want to go downtown, just look around?" I say, "Yeah sure." I'd been in Toronto a lot before, and I said, "Yeah, let's see what's shakin'." And, "Okay, I'll meet you in the lobby in twenty minutes."

We go to the subway, and he's got his watch out. I think he had a pocket watch, I shouldn't wonder. And he's timing the subways, the intervals at which the subways come, and saying, "Hmm, that's interesting. They only have a two-and-a-half-minute interval. That's a lot less than they have in Manhattan!"

And he [Duvivier] always got Cadillacs. The biggest, heaviest, most expensive Cadillacs. And he would drive all over to the gigs in those. He'd never fly. Of course to Europe he had to.

I remember I admired his stamina. We came from some place in Chicago, drove to Indianapolis, played there, and then people came back at this place we played, and we didn't get out of there – you know George had to get his amp, pack up, say goodbye, and *yada yada*, and now it's one o'clock by the time you get on the road. And he would just drive nonstop from Indianapolis to New Jersey. Maybe on the way we'd stop to get a cup of coffee, something like that, but you know, *boom*, he's driving his big fancy Cadillac [*zoom noise*], and we get there at about two o'clock. He drops me off someplace so I can get back to Brooklyn, and he doesn't go back to his pad. He's gotta play that evening.

He was also playing backing up an Italian singer. You have to remember this is some time ago. They still had night clubs in New Jersey. And they had night clubs in Brooklyn. George'd never get any sleep, you know? He had that kind of stamina.

Plowman: Could you tell me a little about Connie Kay? You played with him and George at the same time in Kenny Davern's band.

Grosz: Yes, Connie Kay. I liked Connie, a gentleman. Nice guy. I mean, so was George. And I played with that guy who played with Basie I told you about, Joe Newman.

Connie Kay was a nice guy. Interesting drummer. And he was so happy, even though we [Soprano Summit] were only a five-piece band without a piano, he was so happy to get away from the Modern Jazz Quartet. Because in the Modern Jazz Quartet, for a drummer, there ain't a hell of a lot to do. Everything's real quiet. It was like a crossover jazz group so that sedate people, how would you say, people of breeding, sedate listeners who didn't like a lot of racket and noise…. You could hear the English critic at Royal Albert Hall, "Here we are, twelve hundred people in London, all packed in, reverentially listening to a little man with a little stick hit a little bell." And if you're a drummer, there was just brushes. Which I love brushes, but everything was [whispers] sotto voce. And so he was so happy to get with us.

And he played with Basie. And I don't mean to demean – my job in life is not to put people down, although it's fun [*laughs*]. And I remember, we're recording.

I forgot what it was with Soprano Summit, with two horns, bass, guitar, and drums, no piano. And I'm pumping away [*mimes guitar*] down in the studio, and he's up listening to a playback. And he comes out of the control room, down the stairs, and he says, "Fuck Freddie Green."

He'd played with Basie, and Freddie Green was playing ever more behind the beat, which was not making Connie Kay happy. Or, had not made him happy. He was with us now. And my influences were guys like Eddie Condon, Allan Reuss. And Benny Goodman was one of the few guys, well, most leaders didn't understand what the function of a guitar was. "Just sit over there next to the bass." "Should he sit next to the bass, or the saxophones? Oh okay, next to da bass there." But Benny did. He knew what he wanted. And he told a friend of mine, Steve Jordan, how he wanted it. He said, "The guitar is a musical drum," said Benny Goodman.

And I grew up on guys who hit! It's called a beat. You have a beat. And guitarists and bass players and drummers used to get together and discuss things: "Oh, he plays ahead of the beat, no he plays a little behind, no he plays right in the middle!" You know, they'd get that going. Some bass players play *ba doo bong bong bong* always on top of the beat, always making sort of a nervous feeling. It's good for certain passages. It's like any music. You can't play *placido* all the time. There are passages that require a little heavier hitting, of course. In all music, classical, marches, whatever you're playing. Polkas. And it's no different with jazz. And guys get hooked on just one kind of a sound, and it gets to be a bit boring after a while.

Plowman: And Connie appreciated you for your playing?

Grosz: Yeah, 'cause I like to hit the fuckin' thing. You know? Don't get much chance anymore. But I spent five years playing the banjo. Banjo, in my estimation, except if you're playing with your fingers and you're sitting on a cotton bail [*sings banjo tune*] – banjo, you've got to have a focused attack. You gotta hit the fuckin' thing.

Plowman: And that translated to your guitar playing?

Grosz: Well, to some extent, yes. In fact, at the risk of defaming the gods, I always felt that Eddie Lang sort of played in the middle. He wasn't really a hard...he wasn't really an "on top" player. But he was a *great* player nevertheless. He put the whole rhythm guitar and acoustic guitar, whatever, in jazz, put it on the map. He played the first recorded blues guitar solo in history. In early 1925, with the Mound City Blue Blowers, "12th Street Blues" [*sings blues lick from solo*].

You know who was good, was Teddy Bunn. Teddy Bunn played a regular steel string guitar with his thumb. Even played rhythm with his thumb. And he had a sly, an interesting style. I liked him.

Chet Baker at Nice

Plowman: Could you tell me the story about Chet Baker throwing his trumpet in Nice?

Grosz: Oh yes. Well, the Chet Baker thing. This is in the '70s, shortly after I joined Soprano Summit, with Kenny Davern and Bob Wilber on horns, and George Duvivier on bass. Shortly after I joined that little group, George Wein was managing a jazz festival in Nice, France. Everyone, a lot of people were invited, from all over. There they were, from the States, from Europe, and everywhere else. And so we're playing there, and I have a George Barnes story too, but I don't think that's as interesting.

> [*launches immediately into George Barnes story*]

We had to play with three guitars, George Barnes, myself, and Vinnie Corrao - and briefly, I'm only telling it 'cause it was so strange. So George Barnes, if you don't know who he is, he was a wizard guitar player, and early. He was like a rival to Les Paul. Barnes was a talent. When he was 15, 16 years old he was already playing places in Chicago, playing with mature musicians and so forth. Anyway, in New York he was arguably the busiest studio guitar player. But he knew who Eddie Lang was, and he knew this guy and that guy, you know, he paid attention. He was working with Jimmy McPartland in Chicago, and different bands, as a kid. McPartland was what you would call now, I hate the term Dixieland band, but that's…McPartland was a big Bix Beiderbecke fan, played a lot of those tunes.

So anyway, they had us scheduled for a three-guitar set. Sets were about 45, 50 minutes long. [*laughs*] It's out in the open air, everything is out in the open air, in old Roman ruins that they had fixed up. We're playing along there, and we're all wailing along, and I'm the only guy who doesn't have an amp. They just stick a mic on me. I don't have an electric guitar, I have an acoustic guitar. People don't even know nowadays what that is. And we're playing, I remember playing something like "Love is Just Around the Corner" and Barnes is wailing away, and I'm saying to myself, *Jeez what am I gonna do? This guy is gonna kill us all.* And Vinnie only knew bebop tunes, so he was struggling.

Plowman: [*laughs*]

Grosz: Well, it's true. Barnes was very nice. As the big honcho, he had us sit down before the concert and he had a list of tunes and he said, "Let's make it easy." You know, the tunes everybody knew. "Sunny Side of the Street," you name it, "Honeysuckle Rose," whatever. We're not gonna make history here, we're just gonna get through this set, which is the right way to do it, you know? Don't put musicians into a box. [*grabs chest*] "Oh, shit how does the bridge go? I forgot." "Oh what is this tune? I've never played this tune. How does it go?" You know.

So we're wailing away, and I get the last solo 'cause I'm

Mr. Acoustic, and they get [*claps twice*] a little bit of clap, clap, and all a sudden [*raaahwr*] I get a big hand. And I'm looking, and I'm thinking, *What the f---, what the hell's going on here? I'm not doing anything spectacular.* And Barnes is wondering, and [*laughs*] Vinnie [Corrao]'s looking. At the end of the thing it turned out that because of the French guitar amplifiers – they were different, they couldn't be amplified properly. I came through strong because they had a mic on me. They had mics on the amps of the other guys, you know they stick the mic in front of the amp. Anyway, small incident.

The big incident is, there are quite a few musicians, Zoot Sims...I've let go of their names. We've got a set with Soprano Summit coming up, with Bob Wilber, Kenny Davern and myself, George Duvivier. Who was the drummer, I can't remember. It wasn't Connie Kay on this occasion. I think it was Rosengarden maybe. Yeah, okay. And we're backstage in this open former Roman amphitheater, and in the back they have these heavy – I don't know if they're plastic curtains or something, you have to push them aside to get on stage. Nice is on hills, so in the back you have a ramp. This ramp must have been 50, 60, 70 feet, something like that, to roll up the equipment on and so forth.

So I'm waiting to go on, we're next. Let's say it's two in the afternoon or something. I'm standing around, and George Duvivier says, "Hey Marty, come over here." And I come over and he says, "I want you to meet Benny Carter." [*chuckles nervously*] Benny Carter was one of the gods, one of the luminaries in my constellation. And wow, you know?

I'd shaken Louie Armstrong's hand. That was probably number one.

But anyway, Carter, what a musician. Fantastic. Could play a lot of instruments. He played them all very well, he wrote wonderful arrangements. He was just fantastic. And I've just been introduced to him, and I was basking in the glow of – I'm not a bobby-soxer and autograph collector or anything – but that I would finally have come so far in my life and my career to be on stage and meeting people like this…

Anyway, all of a sudden there's a ruckus from the bandstand. We could hear some kind of noise, something falling over. I don't know what it was. A figure pops out offstage past this sort of heavy curtain that separates us and runs.

And we said, "What the f---, what is this?" We couldn't see. He was really scampering quite fast. And he runs down this ramp, onto the street, and it's obvious he's got a trumpet in his hand. And then he stomps down the street, and they have police around, just to keep the order, move the traffic away. And this cop is standing there, probably bored to tears, French cop. And he's looking at this guy, and says, "What's this?" with a quizzical look on his face.

And the person takes the trumpet and bangs it on the sidewalk. And you can see the valves popping out of it, flying all around. And it turned out to be Chet Baker. And I remembered that because I'd seen Chet Baker before on stage in the US. But you gotta wonder, what the hell's going on here?

What it turned out to be of course – later on it became obvious – is that he was having a kind of a drug episode. And his band, the bunch of people that had been assembled for him, all fine musicians, competent musicians. But Chet was always calling tunes that they'd never heard of. I don't know if they were originals or recorded by one or two people only. You know, "Blue Clouds over Mississippi" or something. "No never heard of it." "The Fat Man Sings." "No, never heard that one either." "The Battery Jump." "No, I never…." You know. And he had some kind of a scene, and he just took his horn and threw it off the stage, ran down, picked it up, and started banging it on the sidewalk. And that was Chet Baker.

He was not a happy person, let's put it that way. I'd seen him come up to the roof. I couldn't sleep, it was Nice, it was warm, it was beautiful, balmy. And the hotel they put us up in, I used to go up to the roof at the end of the evening and sit there and bask in the beautiful summer evening. And he would pop his head out of the elevator with some groupie with him, and he always looked miserable, you know, his mouth turned down at the corners. He had some kind of a big hat on. And he'd take a look around with an expression on his face: "Who are these squares? These creeps?" And then quick he'd pull the girl back into the elevator and they'd go. Maybe he was looking for somebody, some connection and he didn't find it. Had to go someplace else.

Hoagy Carmichael and Wad Allen

Plowman: Can I get the Carnegie Hall with Hoagy Carmichael story? With that sax player with the funny name?

Grosz: So this was at the end of the '70s I guess. It can be looked up. [1979] And there was a gala concert celebrating Hoagy Carmichael, his birthday I think. It was quite impressive. Sudhalter comes over from England with a book that had appeared about Bix written by a record collector. And it had every factoid about Bix in it that you ever wanted to know or didn't want to know. It started off with, like, "Bix Beiderbecke was born on Poplar Street," and literally, "the house had eight windows, the back of the house had six." You know, every detail, and so forth. Anyway, I had to look at the manuscript because somebody wanted to know if I wanted to help write it. Well I wasn't a writer, I hadn't published anything. They asked me because I had made this record called *Hooray for Bix* – which I tried not particularly to imitate Bix in.

So it's the '70s, and we get to the rehearsal and it's quite an assemblage of people. Dave McKenna on piano. And they had Joya Sherrill who had sung with Duke Ellington, and I think she had a show on television or something. Very nice person, very professional. She was gracious and pretty. We had Kay Starr, another very professional, outstandingly convincing vocalist. She could really put it over, Kay. She swung. Well. Jimmy Maxwell on trumpet. Sudhalter was taking lessons from him. It didn't help. [*chuckles*] And then he had, of course, Yank Lawson and Vic Dickenson, Bob Wilber, Dave McKenna, Eddie Miller, a band, you know, four horns and rhythm. A bass player and a drummer who I can't remember – sorry boys.

Anyway, here we are in Carnegie Hall, Hoagy's 80th birthday or something. Yeah, it was going *pro forma*, everybody was doing their thing. And Hoagy is this little man from Indiana who's sort of restless. He appeared to be restless, he was sort of [*fidgets*] one of those guys. Full of pep. And the two things that I remember: Dave McKenna, very interesting piano player, because Dave would do things, interesting things, changing the bass notes on pieces and making medleys, stuff like that. What do you do with a tune like "Lulu's Back in Town"? It's like a dog chasing its tail over and over again. And McKenna had a way of taking tunes like that and making them varied enough to keep you interested, so that by the third chorus you're not saying "check please."

And so McKenna got the job of reading – Dave himself said he was not a great reader. He wasn't like Dick Hyman, he'd be the first to tell you. And he's playing, was it "Washboard Blues"? Or was it "Stardust"? But I think it was "Washboard Blues" if I'm not mistaken. Anyway, McKenna was sweating profusely. His eyes were bloodshot. And I'm looking at McKenna [*laughs*] saying "Oh shit." Somebody had transcribed Hoagy's solo off the record, so he's gotta play the whole thing. And he's schvitzing. And in the middle, Hoagy, in the middle of it, you hear him yell, "That's not half bad!" He's sitting two or three rows back so he can see up on stage.

And then it goes on, there's a big number, what they used to call the breakdown in vaudeville. Everybody on stage, and they're all singing or doing something to "Jubilee." Everybody's going bananas and stuff and half the audience is squeezing out the door so they get a seat at the Russian Tea Room which is next door.

And all of a sudden it's over, and everybody's getting their coats on, and you hear a voice say "HOLD IT, HOLD IT FOLKS, WAIT A MINUTE." And it's Hoagy. And Hoagy walks up to the stage, goes up the stairs, gets the microphone. "I want you to meet a friend of mine. Wad Allen." And this gray-haired guy stands up. "Best slap tongue tenor sax player in Indiana!" And thinking about it now, I wouldn't be surprised if it was scripted. It fit so much the image of Hoagy chewing on a matchstick at the piano with the sleeve garters on.

Plowman: Did Wad play?

Grosz: No, he just got up and said thank you, you know [*laughs*]. He looked like a guy who had been a small-town lawyer or something. He had a suit on. He didn't look like a hick. He had his hair slicked back. You wouldn't know he was from Hoosier territory until he started talking probably. Wad. The final touch, you know? I thought, *Well, typical.*

INTERVIEW 11

Herb Ellis & the Great Guitars

Plowman: Do you have any good stories with Herb Ellis?
Grosz: Herb Ellis was a pleasant…

I had one concert in Canada where the guy who was instrumental in putting it together, somehow liked me. Well, liking somebody is fine, it's nice to be liked. But as a result of this I was put on stage with a group that was prominent in those days called the Great Guitars. At that time it was Herb Ellis, Charlie Byrd and his brother [Joe Byrd] on bass, Barney Kessel, and Joe Pass. Four of them. And the program basically consisted of – each number they'd play the head, that means the beginning, the first chorus, together somehow. They'd sort of slog through that, and then everybody would take solos and each guy was trying to cut the next guy.

Plowman: Who did the comping?
Grosz: Well, all the rest of the guys would all comp and get in each other's way. I mean, it wasn't a very well-rehearsed thing. Once in a while when they had a riff, they'd kinda *ba da loo doot* – they'd all get together on that kind of thing,

Marty with Herb Ellis, 1977

simple stuff. But the rest of it, it was kind of a jumble. I didn't think it was very good. And of course, everybody's trying to cut everybody else. Joe Pass [*imitates guitar theatrics*] and the next guy would come along and [*more guitar theatrics*].

So I remember, they closed the thing. They had a drummer too, can't remember, and Charlie Byrd's brother played one of those Ampeg basses or something. It was like a little stick thing.

Plowman: The worst.

Grosz: Terrible. And he rushed. And we ended the whole thing with "Sweet Georgia Brown," and I get the last solo 'cause I'm acoustic and I get a chorus at the end, you know.

And the guy in the paper the next day – it just sounded like a panic in a bird house at the zoo. In those days, in jazz concerts, Jersey jazz had a thing where they had like eight pianos on stage, all playing at the same time. What are you gonna get out of that? You're gonna get a good photo op, but that's about it. The music is gonna be crazy. Insanity.

And so it was with these four guitars and me. It's nuts. I just stayed back and played rhythm. They gave me a solo, and I did a very simple thing. The next day the newspaper columnist wrote *Well, it was a lot of playing, and the only thing that made sense was...*my playing something at least. Not, you know [*mimes guitar wizardry*], all these guys trying to out-virtuoso one another. Which usually meant playing as many notes as you could on guitar. Like piano, you know? Running water all the time.

Plowman: What were the guys like?

Grosz: The guys? Joe Pass wasn't interested. He was kind of, I would think he was a bit difficult. I don't know how to say it. Was he arrogant? I don't know. He wasn't [*puts on a friendly tone*] "Hi! Yeah, oh yeah! I'm looking forward to hearing you!" That wasn't Joe Pass. Eh, you know. And Herb Ellis and Barney Kessel were nice, and Charlie Byrd, okay, later on I did a week with him at the Maryland thing. He did his thing, I did my thing, we did one number each night together. Took care of it that way. And that was okay, you know?

One night it just struck me, what people think is show biz. Are people really impressed by that kind of stuff? Are people really impressed by seeing five trumpet players on stage at the same time? I remember somebody had written out, harmonized, Bunny Berigan's chorus on "I Can't Get Started" or "Marie" or something, and four trumpets playing it. Well, four trumpets playing it, it's like those Supersax recordings where five saxophones are playing harmonized Charlie Parker solos. Here's Charlie Parker, who's like a bird in the sky, wheeling like a pigeon, you know? Making all kinds of turns and squiggles and all of a sudden – this pigeon weighs two hundred pounds.

[*Both laugh*]

Grosz: Did I say the right thing?

That was the premise of the Louis Armstrong tour I did of Europe, with three trumpets playing harmonized Louis Armstrong solos. Braff got out of it, he was on the show too, but he had a little spot for himself. Well, that's the way they think, you know. "Oh what's happening today?" "Well, we've got six basses on stage!"

Plowman: I haven't had to be a part of one of those yet. Maybe someday that'll happen.

Grosz: I don't think so.

Plowman: Yeah it seems the most unlikely category.

Grosz: Well jazz concerts are over, so....

CREDITS

Except as noted below, all images are from the author's private collection and are included courtesy of the author.

INDEX

ABOUT THE AUTHOR

Marty Grosz is considered among the best acoustic jazz guitarists of the twentieth century, as well as a vocalist, humorist, composer and arranger.

The son of celebrated German expressionist George Grosz, Marty was born in Berlin in 1930 and came to the United States at age three. He has performed with jazz greats such as Herb Ellis, Charlie Byrd, Ruby Braff, Dick Hyman, Leroy "Slam" Stewart, Bob Haggart, George Duvivier, Bob Wilber, and Kenny Davern.

Beginning in the 1950s, Marty became a prominent figure of Chicago's jazz club scene and toured with the New York Jazz Repertory Orchestra, Soprano Summit, The Classic Jazz Quartet, and the Orphan Newsboys.

Having played everywhere from the White House to Carnegie Hall, Marty lives and performs in Philadelphia.

Marty can be reached at marty.grosz@goldenalleypress.com and facebook.com/marty.grosz

CPSIA information can be obtained
at www.ICGtesting.com
Printed in the USA
LVHW081619030920
664945LV00036B/2753